Where Is Ana Mendieta?

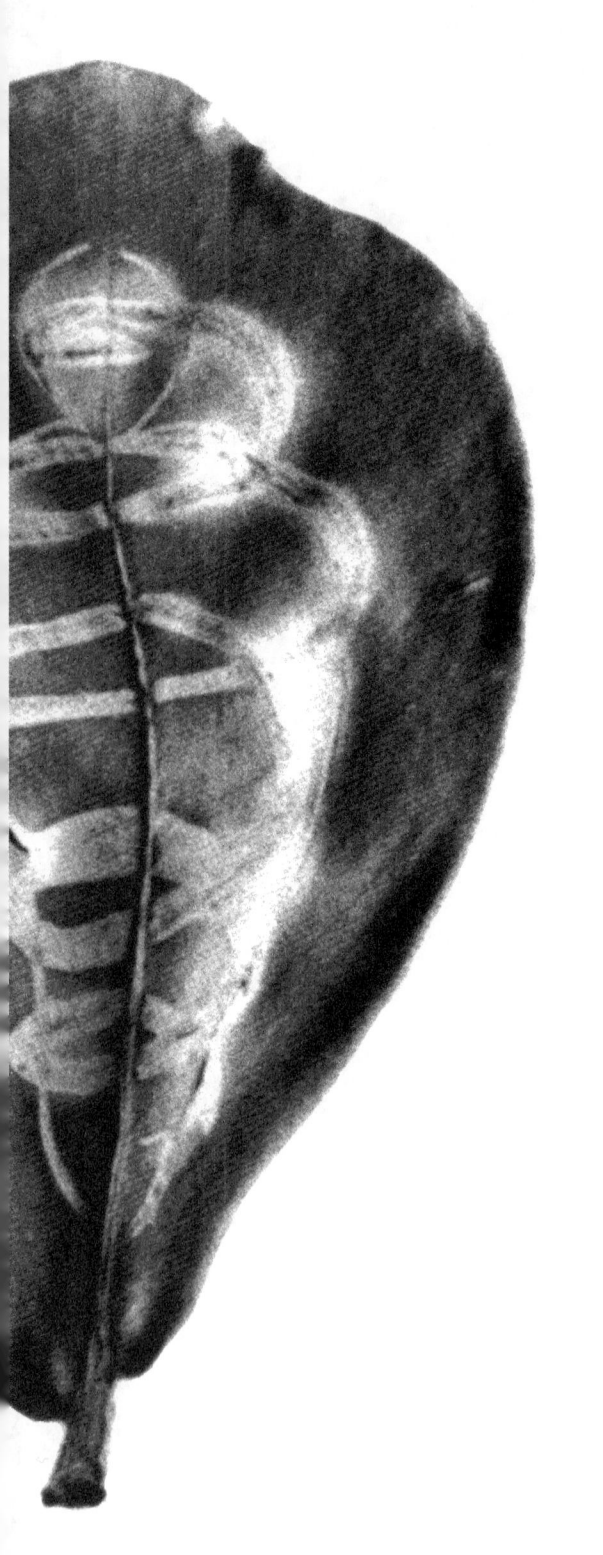

Where Is

JANE BLOCKER

Ana Mendieta?

Identity, Performativity, and Exile

Duke University Press   Durham and London   1999

© 1999 Duke University Press
All rights reserved
Title page: Ana Mendieta, untitled, 1982–84, detail.
Designed by Amy Ruth Buchanan
Typeset in Joanna by Tseng Information Systems, Inc.
Library of Congress Cataloging-in-Publication Data
appear on the last printed page of this book.

For Roger

CONTENTS

LIST OF ILLUSTRATIONS

PREFACE

Ana Mendieta's ashes are buried in my hometown. Such is my relationship to her. She moved there before I did, and, although we lived there at the same time, she moved away again before I had ever heard of her. She received two degrees in art from the University of Iowa eight years before I began my art degree there. When her father was released from prison and emigrated to the United States, he was asked to speak to my eleventh-grade Spanish class about his experiences. Although I was profoundly affected by his description of prison life, I did not remember his name until I began researching this project. Both he and my Spanish teacher have since passed away. I visited New York for the first time a few months before Ana Mendieta's death. By the time I was truly aware of Ana Mendieta the artist, I had already moved away from Iowa to live in Chicago, and she had already been killed and buried in Cedar Rapids. I have followed her unwittingly and become separated from her unknowingly for over two decades. She knew people I know, went places I went, grew up in the same landscape, entered the same institutions. Although the paths of our lives intersect at certain points, I did not know her.

ACKNOWLEDGMENTS

Carol Mavor once told me that my biggest fault is my absolute inability to accept a compliment. I fear not only that she is right but that I am incapable of giving one effectively either. No doubt the problem is owing to the admixture of a strong sentimental streak and a Germanic stoicism, which, when combined, make me either silent about praise or sloppily tearful. This I blame directly on my parents, who at least had the good sense to give me a more useful legacy, a respect for education and a strong interest in scholarship and writing. I share this legacy with my sisters and brother, who are equally uncomfortable about recognition, but who perhaps deserve it more than I. Most useful in this project has been their unwarranted assumption that I would finish it.

Perhaps my trouble also lies with Carol Mavor herself, who has so showered me with compliments that I can hardly take it anymore. I once told her that the single defining feature of her character is excess, but it is hardly a fault to be excessively kind, generous, intelligent, open, and, yes, complimentary. One of Carol's most generous acts was to share Della Pollock with me. Della has both complimented and complemented my writing on an embarrassing number of occasions by gracefully editing and rephrasing it while pretending that I was the source of its efficacy.

There are other people, too, of course, who helped make this book possible. Joy Kasson and Tomoko Masuzawa had everything to do with the completion of my dissertation, from which this book developed. They are, like Carol and Della, acrobats who make teaching and writing look so easy that soon one finds oneself in traction for having tried to imitate their acts unsupervised. Mame Jackson is another contortionist I know, and I will need a lifetime to learn her tricks for leadership, friendship, and optimism.

I have many friends and colleagues who didn't really have much to do with this book directly but who helped me think or kept me happy or both: Isabela Basombrio, who is clever and keenly critical; Nancy Jones, who isn't afraid of anything and tells a good joke when you need it; Terry Kerby, who let me hide in her office from any number of unpleasant encounters, including writing this book; Amy Buchanan, who saved my life in New York; Nahum Chandler, who restored my faith; Kate Anderson, who is deeply beautiful; my students at Wayne State, who taught me so much and pretended to laugh at my bad jokes; and the entire Lindsay family, which has been the source of great joy for over a decade.

There are several people whom I don't really know but who generously offered me their time anyway: Raquel Mendieta, Nancy Spero, B. Ruby Rich, Mañuel Pardo, Cecile Panzieri, and an unknown number of librarians in at least three states. I am also grateful for the financial support of the Luce Foundation in American Art of the American Council of Learned Societies and the W. Hawkins Ferry Endowment at Wayne State University.

This book is for my grandparents and my Great Aunt Jane, all of whom passed away while I was writing it. As Jane would have said, they were the berries. It is also for Roger Lindsay, to whom I owe everything that matters.

Where Is Ana Mendieta?

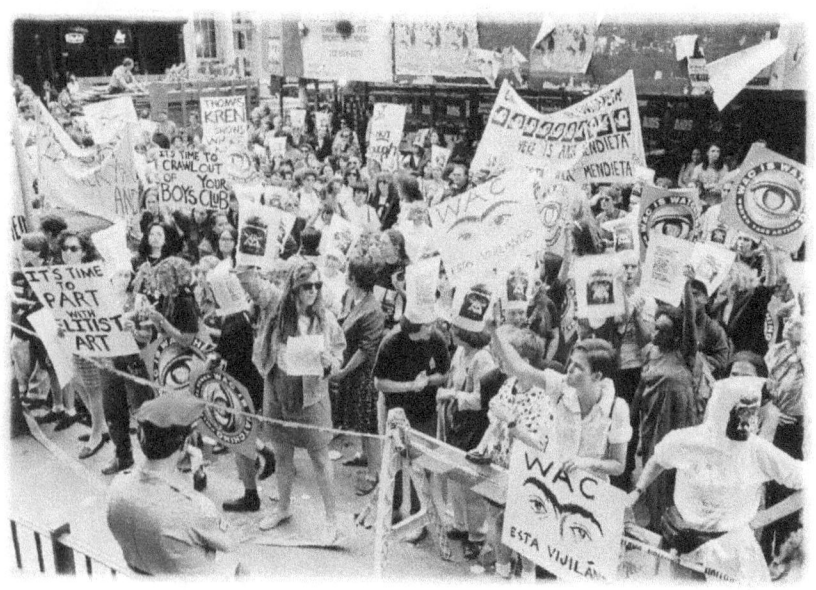

Plate 1. Women's Action Coalition protest, New York, 25 June 1992. Photograph courtesy of Lisa Kahane.

Introduction

WHERE IS ANA MENDIETA?

I can not forget this death. I can not forget the dehumanization of men that causes the brutalization of women. I can not forget the inhumanity of a society that will not recognize that the oppression of one member of that society by another hurts us all. I can not forget that this is what we fear every day. —Betsy Damon, "In Homage to Ana Mendieta"

In June 1992, on the day the new Guggenheim Museum in SoHo opened its inaugural exhibition, five hundred protesters gathered in front of the museum, a small group among them holding a banner that said, "Carl Andre is in the Guggenheim. Where is Ana Mendieta? ¿Donde está Ana Mendieta?" (pl. 1).[1] In addition to this gathering outside the museum, some protesters managed to get into its invitation-only gala and drop copies of a photograph of Mendieta's face onto Andre's floor sculptures. Some of the demonstrators wore T-shirts with this photograph printed on the back.[2] The demonstration was organized primarily by the Women's Action Coalition because the museum's exhibition featured only one female artist with four white male artists and because Carl Andre, Ana Mendieta's accused killer, was among them.[3]

Ana Mendieta was born in Havana in 1948, was forced into exile in the United States in 1961, married minimalist sculptor Carl Andre in 1985, and died tragically later that year. Andre's defense attorneys claimed that she fell or jumped from his thirty-fourth-story apartment in Manhattan; the prosecution said that he pushed her. Although he was acquitted of her murder in February 1988, there were many who still believed at the time of this protest that he was guilty.[4] The protest staged in front of the Guggenheim was a response to a variety of injustices: not just the exclusion of women from an art museum, but their persistent absence from a wide range of domains of power; not just the marginalization of people of color, symbolized by Ana Mendieta, but the seeming institutional sanction of a judicial verdict that pronounced Andre innocent of having killed her.

The question on the banner held up by the protesters—"Where is Ana Mendieta?"—is rhetorical; that is, it asks for but does not really want an answer. The one literal answer—that she is dead and her ashes buried in Cedar Rapids, Iowa—is painfully dissatisfying. By asking where she is, the demonstrators are really asking where she is not. Location and dislocation are laminated, mutually sustaining, sometimes indistinguishable sources of power. Thus, the strength of the question lies in the fact that it makes palpable, indeed, demands a space for, Mendieta's incoherence and illegibility within the terms of the exhibition. It performatively reproduces her absence and makes her an elusive and powerful figure. No one asks, "Where is Carl Andre?" because it is presumed that we know all too well. Andre is in the Guggenheim, which is to say that he is securely established in gender, racial, aesthetic, and institutional traditions. His identity is reduced to a simple tautology that makes him nakedly legible, lays bare his privilege. He is (to use Peggy Phelan's twist on Simone de Beauvoir) "marked," while Mendieta remains "unmarked."[5]

The powerful indeterminacy of this question makes it interesting to me. In asking it, one simultaneously demands and forecloses an answer. Therefore, by asking the question, the protesters have neatly summarized the central paradox of writing about this artist. With it, they effectively articulate the common perception that, despite nearly twenty-five years of critical success and worldwide exposure, Mendieta is missing. The catalog edited by Gloria Moure that accompanied Mendieta's recent one-woman exhibition in Spain gives voice to the pervasive (if problematic) desire to find her. It makes the strong claim that the exhibition "*rescues from oblivion a body of work that deserves the recognition of public and critics alike.*"[6]

To what degree can Mendieta, about whom scores of reviews, articles, and catalogs have been written, whose work has been shown in over a hundred exhibitions around the world, be in need of such rescue? To what degree is she in peril of being forgotten?

The answer is complex. Certainly, the monstrous way in which she died and the sense of raw injustice that persists as a result of it suggest that no amount of celebrity, exposure, critical acclaim, or financial success is enough. Remembrance is a process, not a task to be completed; it is carried out through constant repetition and renewal. To be satisfied that Mendieta has been sufficiently memorialized is to admit, finally, that she is gone. "Where?" serves as a living reminder rather than a stone marker for that loss.

It is not simply out of mourning, however, that the sense of Mendieta's dis-location persists. The SoHo protest made it clear that she is tied up with a great many things whose regular disappearance from the art world is mystifying, shocking, and enervating. It was very difficult to believe that, in 1992, after twenty years of feminist art, after the advent of poststructural critiques of power, after the pluralization of media and the politicization of message, the Guggenheim could so unapologetically set forth its myopic vision of modern art. It was thus hardly surprising when, five years later, in January 1997, *Artnews* published a list of "the fifty most powerful people in the art world," which included only six women and one nonwhite man.[7] The politics of backlash remind feminists that gender equality is neither simple nor final. The successful visibility of any female artist in this context must be met with skeptical questions: For whose benefit is this success, and for how long? In an era of such political insecurity, "Where?" can be a powerful weapon against a world map, hastily redrawn in light of new postmodern "discoveries," in which feminism and multiculturalism are officially approved tourist attractions.

Ana Mendieta's short life, aesthetic choices, gender, ethnicity, and politics have contributed to her absence from a variety of discursive sites. I am drawn to the question, "Where is Ana Mendieta?" not only because it interrogates her absence, but also because it reveals the willful refusal to appear as an act of transgression. Mendieta has been a victim of normative mapping that, by gerrymandering or simple elimination, has made her unrepresentable. As a consequence, however, she has also escaped to some degree the limitations of these territorial disputes. The question is thus useful because it points to Mendieta as a subject produced discursively by questions of location. By asking, "Where?" and being unable definitively to provide an answer, this question places Mendieta in motion, thwarting the logic of fixed categories, yet making space for alternative identifications.

The question is a metaphor for the very task of writing this book or any other historically driven analysis. "Where is Ana Mendieta?" also means, Where can history locate her?—when *locate* means both "accidentally to find" and "intentionally to position." Can she be found hermeneutically in her works of art? Can her works help reconstruct her complex identity, or can they be used to limit the categories by which identity itself is defined? What investments, conscious or unconscious, do historians bring to the work of finding her?

My project here is twofold. I want first to locate Mendieta within art history, to find a place for her art, her ethnicity, her nationality, and her gender. I will sketch her relation to the complex forces of conceptual and earth art, postminimalism and feminism, critical theory and performance art, to claim that her work makes a significant contribution to postmodern critical practice. By *postmodern* I mean specifically the theoretical disputation of the terms of difference and identity, the analysis of subjectivity and authority, and the reconceptualization of history. At the same time, however, I want to recognize the inherent limitations of fixing her location. I will read what has been written about Mendieta considering how it has been shaped by competing aesthetic, sexual, racial, and nationalist ideologies. I will also suggest that, at this critically fertile moment, when we are just beginning to see more extensive and intellectually challenging accounts of Mendieta's life and work, it is crucial to understand the means by which she confounds historiography. That is, I hope to posit an answer while at the same time clinging to the indeterminacy of the question.

LOSING A DECADE

> I want to say something of what I believe has been repressed in the almost universal tendency, in the art world of the 1980s, to "lose" an entire decade—the 1970s—as a period in which "nothing" happened. —Victor Burgin, *The End of Art Theory*

The "nothing" that happened in the 1970s was vividly staged by Vito Acconci in his 1971 videotaped performance *Claim*. Paranoid, psychotic, victimized, isolated, masculine, fearful, Acconci personified every troubling and exalted attribute of the modern artist. Staged at the bottom of a flight of stairs in the basement of a loft at 93 Grand Street in New York, the three-hour performance featured Acconci sitting blindfolded, holding a lead pipe (which he occasionally wielded), and muttering to himself, "I've got to do this. I've got to stay down here. I can't let anyone down here." As the performance droned on to the point that Acconci was exhausted and hoarse, various gallery visitors descended the stairs to have a look. The tedious nothingness of the long performance was punctuated by explosive moments when Acconci turned his wound-up tension to savage anger, jumping from his chair, swinging his weapon wildly, and whacking the stair steps and railing. The violence had a comic aspect, however, since gallerygoers easily dodged his blind aggression. One viewer actually prodded him with an umbrella as though he were a caged animal being roused by an audience eager for a controlled display of brutishness. In the context of the lingering Vietnam War, *Claim* provided a shiver of recognition: an isolated and frightened man violently attempts to claim a territory, the limits and worth of which he cannot see, against an enemy whom he does not know, and in front of a video audience that consumes violence.

Acconci's performance is emblematic of the lost decade of the 1970s. It is exemplary of the art that Victor Burgin characterizes as having been repressed.[8] Its medium reflects an era of intense artistic experimentation in which artists, inflamed over the economic involvement of art institutions in the Vietnam War, distrustful of the commodification of art, or angered by the racism, sexism, and elitism of gallery and museum exhibitions, tested a variety of ways to democratize and disseminate the art experience.[9] Conceptual art, earthworks, installations, video, body art, and performance all worked actively to redefine the spaces in which art was viewed and to integrate the audience into the process of artistic production. Ana Mendieta and her contemporaries worked to disrupt the authority of the artist and to eliminate the art object. Victor Burgin has described this cherished goal as the desire to make "the present absent."[10]

Acconci's title, *Claim*, reflexively asserts the uncertainty of various border claims, including those that were developing between modernism and nascent postmodernism. *Claim* dramatized this emerging indistinction. Its confrontational staging also reflected and was reflected in the territorial disputes erupting throughout the decade: the violence between students and the National Guard at Kent State; the struggles between participants on all sides of the women's liberation movement; the Stonewall riots and the reactionary violence that followed; the continued skirmishes over civil and economic rights and racial equality; the tensions between the people and a corrupt government.

Another significant characteristic of the 1970s lay just beneath the surface of its artistic diversity and progressive public battles. The more private repression to which Burgin refers—both psychological and political, both philosophical and real—took root alongside the liberatory aspects of the decade and came to full flower in the 1980s. In 1976, the Trilateral Commission, a consortium of intellectuals and political leaders from the United States, Europe, and Japan, released a report in which Samuel Huntington, Harvard professor and adviser to the White House, warned against the "excess of democracy" that had been exhibited in the protests and civil disobedience of the 1960s. Huntington recommended strict limitations on the exercise of popular politics.[11] The federal government subsequently implemented a variety of measures meant to make it harder to participate in grassroots organizations, to delimit the gains made by the activism that had already occurred, and to isolate groups that had formerly worked in coalition.[12] For the art world, this reactionary trend (which disguised itself as merely a corrective against what it characterized as 1960s extremism) manifested itself in two ways: neoconservative aesthetics and the selective elimination of women, nonwhites, and homosexuals from official memory.

To the extent that this period's aesthetic can be defined by lack—lack of authorial privilege, lack of commodity, lack of objecthood, lack of permanence, and lack of celebrity—it troubled the critical and aesthetic conventions of modernism. The 1980s misplaced the previous decade because that decade's democratic aspirations seemed excessive to the institutionalized avant-garde. Performance art and the other new media have no intrinsic worth as commodifiable objects; they are meaningful only in the actions of their audience and in the memory of their fleeting existence. Laura Trippi and Gary Sangster note that the 1980s "may be remembered as a decade marked by strategic, and often magnificent, lapses of memory." "Propelled in part by growing interest in the investment potential of contemporary art," they claim, "the eighties were marked by a diversionary return to traditional media and methods. Almost with a vengeance, painting and sculpture reappeared."[13]

The aesthetic backlash against the performativity of alternative media began early in the 1980s, as Douglas Crimp points out, with exhibitions like "Documenta 7" (1982) that rededicated themselves to displaying painting and sculpture and reintroducing formalist analysis. Rudi Fuchs, the curator of "Documenta 7," said at a press conference that "the time one can show contemporary art in makeshift spaces, converted factories and so on, is over. Art is a noble achievement and it should be handled with dignity and respect. Therefore we have finally built real walls." Crimp decries the reactionary treatment of site-specific conceptual art using Christy Rupp's *Rat Patrol* (1979) as an example of "one of those art practices, now fairly numerous, that makes no concessions to the institutions of exhibition, even deliberately confounds them. As a result, it cannot be understood by most people as art, for only exhibition institutions can, at this historical juncture, fully legitimate any practice as art."[14] Crimp's contentions remind us that conservative politics and increasing market speculation prohibit the inclusion of Acconci's performance (along with a legion of other conceptual, earth art, body art, or performance pieces) in the realm of fine art.

More important, Crimp argues convincingly that, even when such works are granted a place and are squeezed in amid the pages of dominant art histories, their power is diminished by the conservative aesthetic philosophies in the context of which they are discussed. The radical politics of much twentieth-century art (even that which appears in more traditional media) can be safely managed and neutralized by forcing it into narratives of progress or the masterpiece and into categories by medium, categories that, by definition, impose a formalist critical framework. Therefore, when we ask, "Where is this decade?" and, "Where are these media?" it is crucial that we understand the paradoxical value of their exclusion: the power of remaining unmarked by the mythologies of art institutions.

Crimp is keen to impress on his reader the idea that historical inclusion is sometimes only a form of co-optation by a historical model that may not only go unchallenged but be variously and repeatedly reinforced. To the extent that the avant-garde is overtaken by uninspected conservatism, we cannot assume that even revolutionary practices are free of their own repressions. Even while these excluded sites, these marginal media and unsalable practices, are taken up, they leave behind still further exclusions. The "loss" of the 1970s is, as Joseph Roach might say, an instance of "careful forgetting" behind which lie not only aesthetic bias but entrenched sexism.[15] In addition to that decade's forays into alternative media, it is notable because it marks the most prolific production of feminist art and theory in history. At the heart of the decade, however, lies a hole, a vacant center: the troubling nothingness of the feminine.

Carolee Schneemann dramatized the anxieties that proliferate in response to that hole in her celebrated performance *Interior Scroll*, staged in 1975 and again in 1977. The performance cast Schneemann as both artist and object. She appeared naked on stage (the familiar nude artist's model) and then began stroking her body with paint. She proceeded slowly to pull from her vagina a scroll, from which she read aloud:

> I met a happy man
> a structuralist filmmaker . . .
> he said we are fond of you
> you are charming
> but don't ask us
> to look at your films
> we cannot
> there are certain films
> we cannot look at
> the personal clutter
> the persistence of feelings . . .
> he said you can do as I do
> take one clear process
> follow its strictest
> implications intellectually
> establish a system of
> permutations establish
> their visual set. . . .
>
> he protested
> you are unable to appreciate
> the system the grid
> the numerical rational
> procedures—
> the Pythagorean cues—
>
> I saw my failings were worthy
> of dismissal I'd be buried
> alive my works lost. . . .[16]

The genius of Schneemann's performance lies in the fact that it exposes supposedly unpoliticized aesthetics as a cover for sexism. The appeal to minimalism, clarity, process, rationality, and purity in a good deal of both modernist and postmodernist art theory is the public side of a private inability to see women as artists at all.

To dismantle modernism, then, meant aggressively to question sexism, to expose the mechanisms of identity and difference, and to deconstruct representation. Indeed, the efficacy of postmodernism is often said to lie in its feminist conscience. As Lucy Lippard wrote in 1980, "Feminism's greatest contribution to the future of art has probably been precisely its lack of contribution to modernism." [17] Pulling the scroll from her vagina, Schneemann calmly clarifies the situation: it is not her art but her body that is the problem. The Lacanian metaphors proliferate ridiculously. Just as with sexual difference, in the 1970s there is "nothing to see and nothing to hide." [18]

It was among these competing claims that Ana Mendieta was trained and later worked. Her art is characterized by the same experimentation, dissolubility, feminist consciousness, and identity politics as appear (in various proportions) in the work of Acconci, Schneemann, Robert Morris, Cindy Sherman, and Eleanor Antin. It was buoyed by the decade's exciting artistic activity and put at risk of being buried by the decade's sexist and racist repressions. If the 1970s is now difficult to find because its innovations have failed to meet the demands of profitability, how much more elusive is the artist whose gender and ethnicity placed her on the margins of this margin? Even more troubling questions, however, are prompted by Schneemann's performance: What kind of cosmetic makeover must be endured in order to be found? Maybe it is better not to answer when they ask, "Where?" because to do so would mean using their maps.

MAPMAKING

Why is it, exactly at the moment when so many of us who have been silenced begin to demand the right to name ourselves, to act as subjects rather than objects of history, that just then the concept of subjecthood becomes "problematic?"
—Nancy Harstock, "Rethinking Modernism"

No doubt the 1970s' vogue for democratizing the art-making process was influenced by the greater availability in English of French poststructuralist theory. Roland Barthes's famous essay "The Death of the Author," for example, dismissed the tendency in literary studies to privilege the author over the reader. [19] The deification of the author, he suggested, was a product of an outmoded modernist ideology rooted in capitalism and positivism. The death that Barthes made famous was simply another disappearance, another manifestation of the oblivion for which the 1970s is infamous. In a sense, Acconci performs this death by making the relative power of artist and audience the subject of his work. Just as Barthes argued in the case of literature, Acconci's *Claim* is actuated by the viewer, whose presence is both threatening and necessary. The visionary artist, exalted by modernist philosophers Wassily Kandinsky and Wilhem Worringer, is now blind and subterranean.

Artists and critics of the period (such as Michael Fried, Victor Burgin, Frank Popper, and Lucy Lippard) wrote in diverse ways and contexts about the diminishment of the artist's authority and the narrowing of the gap between art and life. Popper explains how the process of overturning the authorial hierarchy took place: "The 'work of art' itself has more or less disappeared by gradual stages. The artist has taken upon himself new functions which are more like those of an intermediary than a creator, and has begun to enunciate open-ended environmental propositions and hypotheses. Finally the spectator has been impelled to intervene in the aesthetic process in an unprecedented way."[20] Despite the important effect that it had on the history of art, the dematerialization of the art object was accompanied by a set of unexamined assumptions: that the work of art had been and could be viewed as distinct from the identity of the artist who made it; that all artists had equal access to the authority that this movement sought to diminish; that an attempt to subvert that authority in an artistic context would not be recuperated by larger cultural claims to dominance; that *spectators* can refer to an undifferentiated group whose subjectivity is clear and whose access to works of art is equal.

From her earliest days as a student at the University of Iowa to the time of her death, Mendieta followed the fundamental directives of 1970s art making as summarized by Popper: to eliminate the object, to subvert the artist's authority, and to involve the viewer more actively. She adapted and synthesized the artistic trends of the decade—conceptualism, body art, performance, installations, and earth art—to animate the territorial boundaries between artist and audience, male and female, body and spirit. In each instance, however, by virtue of her identity and her politics, she exposed and troubled the assumptions that lie hidden behind those directives. Her work challenges the philosophers of dematerialization to imagine more complex and extensive models of authority, more diverse constituencies, and more sophisticated concepts of identity and subjectivity.

By repeatedly turning her own body into an art object, Mendieta took part in the 1970s trend in which the artist's physical self became both image and medium. Originally, this trend was associated with such male artists of the mid-1960s as Yves Kline, Bruce Nauman, Dennis Oppenheim, and Vito Acconci; the latter in particular was informed by Maurice Merleau-Ponty's phenomenology. The trend was later taken over by women artists working in the 1970s who saw it as an expedient way to examine female subjectivity and identity. This is exemplified in Mendieta's oeuvre by such works as *Glass on Body* (1972), where she photographed her own face, breasts, thighs, hips, and buttocks as she manipulated and squeezed them against sheets of glass, through which her distorted features appeared grotesque (pl. 2).

Glass on Body is comparable to a 1969 film by Bruce Nauman called *Pulling Mouth* in which Nauman is "engaged in the rules by which the body is expressive" (pl. 3).[21] Nauman uses a slow-motion film to document and exaggerate his contorted face making. The two pieces share the influence of conceptualism: each is a simple experiment, or process, of limited duration using the human body. They differ, however, by the sexed signification of that body. Nauman's work, like that of other men at the time, presented the artist's body as a closed system, an object of perceptual interest, or a signifier of universal humanness. Mendieta's work, like that of other feminist performance artists, interrogated the ideology of gender and the female body as a field of masculine control.[22] Mendieta's manipulation of her own malleable flesh against the glass and the resulting carnivalesque perversion of her once recognizable figure turn body art toward such feminist issues as the normative construction of beauty and the female body as monstrous other.

Mendieta's M.A. thesis project pushed the examination of gender identity and physical appearance further still (pl. 4). Mendieta asked her friend Morty Sklar to shave off his beard, after which she transferred the hair to her own face, thus transforming herself conceptually into a man.[23] This piece was similar in some respects to the "drag" performances of a number of her female contemporaries, including Eleanor Antin, Martha Wilson, Annette Messager, Adrian Piper, and Jacki Apple. Antin's *The King* (1973), in which she attempted to experience life as a man by wearing a heavy beard and mustache, is an obvious example (pl. 5).

On a superficial level, Mendieta's work is also comparable to Vito Acconci's *Conversions* series (1971), in which he underwent a temporary "sex change" by burning off the hair on his chest, manipulating his pectorals to produce breasts, and hiding his penis between his legs. Yet the meanings of such gender-crossing performances are determined by extremely different relation to the body and to the relative power that it encodes. Acconci's access to this momentary experience of "femininity" is enabled by his privilege as a man to explore and appropriate the feminine. The interpretation of works like his is, moreover, biased by assumptions about the distinct motives of male and female artists.

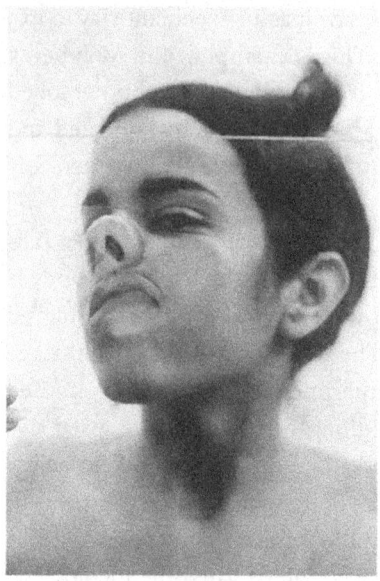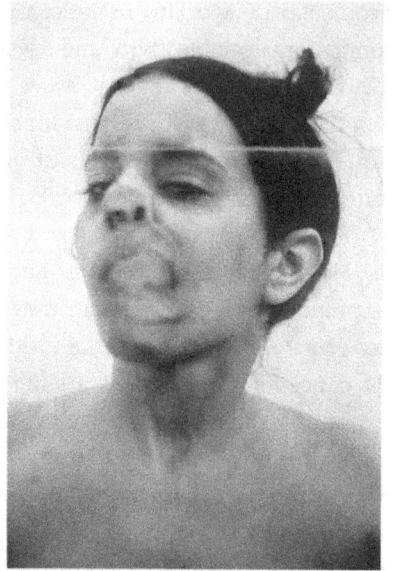

Lucy Lippard points out that "when women use their own faces and bodies they are immediately accused of narcissism. . . . Because women are considered sex objects, it is taken for granted that any woman who presents her nude body in public is doing so because she thinks she is beautiful. She is a narcissist, and Acconci, with his less romantic image and pimply back is an artist."[24] The female body remains the most consistent feature of Mendieta's oeuvre. It appears in sculptural, physical, and photographic form and dominates her *Tree of Life, Fetish, Silueta, Sand Woman,* and *Leaf Drawing* series. The charge of narcissism has legitimized the assumption that her work has only personal significance as a therapeutic response to traumatic expatriation. For example, critics have suggested that Mendieta's work is a "personal investigation of the nature of being," a reflection of her "innermost feelings on life," or a "personal dialogue with nature, which represents the land she didn't have."[25] Such characterizations are an effective means of marginalizing and feminizing her work.

While modernist rhetoric tends to privilege the personal expression of the artist as the register of dramatic cultural trends, the rhetoric surrounding Mendieta typically limits the significance of her expression to her experience alone. It suggests that the meaning of her art is contained by the particularities of her own life rather than by larger political and cultural contexts and questions. This approach relies on the depoliticized notion of the *personal*, according to which both the artist and her work are

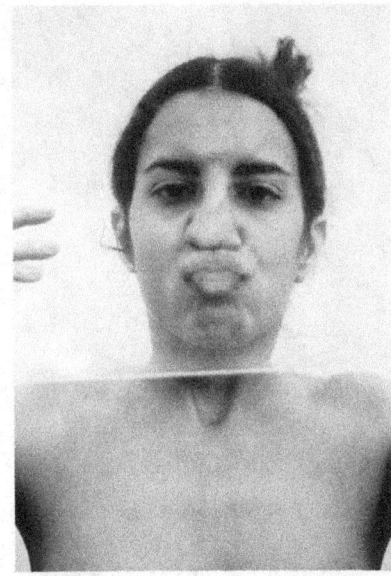

Plate 2. Ana Mendieta, *Glass on Body*, 1972. Color photographs of performance at the University of Iowa. Courtesy of the Estate of Ana Mendieta and Galerie Lelong, New York.

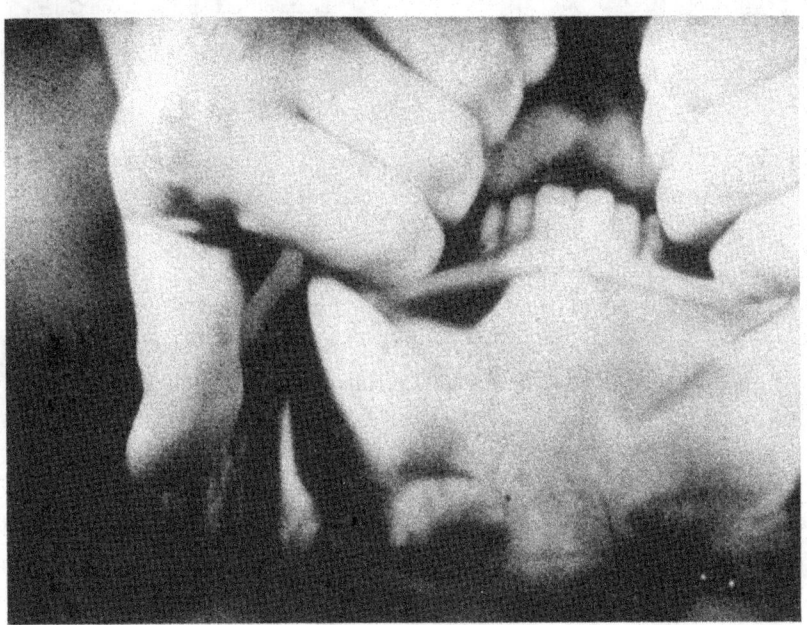

Plate 3. Bruce Nauman, *Pulling Mouth*, 1969. Slow-motion film, 16 millimeter, black and white, silent, 9 minutes. Courtesy of the artist.

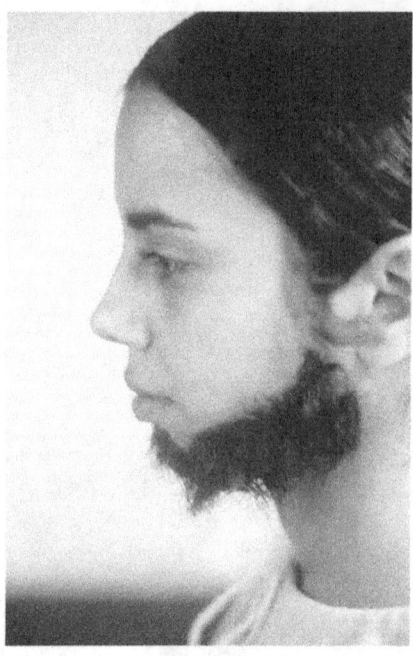

Plate 4. Ana Mendieta, *Facial Hair Transplant*, 1972. Color photograph documenting performance at the University of Iowa. Courtesy of the Estate of Ana Mendieta and Galerie Lelong, New York.

presumed to be in some ways unknowable, the critical importance of the work is limited, and the identity of its creator is self-evident.

The most recent and easily most egregious example of this phenomenon appears in an analysis by Donald Kuspit. Kuspit psychoanalyzes Mendieta through her works, presuming to see in them a traumatic first sexual experience, a dysfunctional mother/daughter relationship, and, ultimately, a desire for the father. He follows the most clichéd protocols of psychotherapy, first by recognizing symptoms, then by pronouncing a diagnosis. "Mendieta," he writes, "clearly had a troubled sense of self, as her very self-centered art—in which there are not only no men, but no other women—suggests. Her trouble had to do with her relationship with her mother and various mother surrogates." The solipsism of which he accuses Mendieta is gender specific. Moreover, it bespeaks a profound sense of threat: "Mendieta preferred to have narcissistic intercourse with Mother Earth than sexual intercourse with man." Despite his professed sympathy for Mendieta's victimization as a woman and for her desire to escape male sexual domination, Kuspit pathologizes Mendieta's sexuality as narcissistic and geophilic. Kuspit concludes in a footnote that "Mendieta was not as liberated or enlightened—feminist—as she may have thought she was." [26]

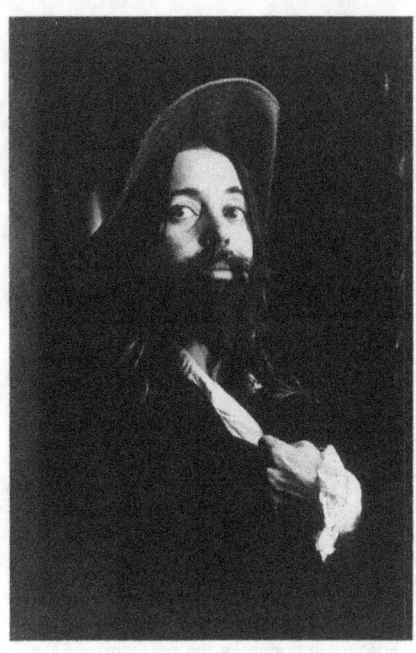

Plate 5. Eleanor Antin, *The King*, 1973. Videotaped performance. Photo courtesy of Ronald Feldman Fine Arts, New York.

Kuspit's diagnostic procedure allows him to ignore the political critique that underpins a great deal of Mendieta's work and the feminist milieu in which it was created. Perhaps the most well known of Mendieta's body pieces/performances was done in response to the rape and murder of a female student at the University of Iowa in 1972. Angered by the violence of patriarchal culture, Mendieta invited colleagues to a "performance" at a designated place in a wooded area near campus. Once there, the "audience" discovered Mendieta lying half naked, facedown in the grass, her clothing torn, and her legs covered with stage blood all too convincingly applied (pl. 6).[27] While many male artists experimented with the unfamiliar experience of making themselves the object of the viewer's gaze, female artists worked to expose the violence and control that can lie behind the gaze, which for them (us) is neither novel nor escapable. The overt politics of this piece was later echoed in the work of Suzanne Lacy and Leslie Labowitz, whose *Three Weeks in May* (1977) attempted to visualize the hidden violence of rape that Los Angeles police and city officials, passive to gender politics, could not see.

Kuspit's work, and other work like it, rests on an unquestioned male/female dichotomy. Through its corrosive judgment, it participates in what Adrienne Rich has called "compulsory heterosexuality": the system of regulatory procedures by which normative heterosexuality is maintained

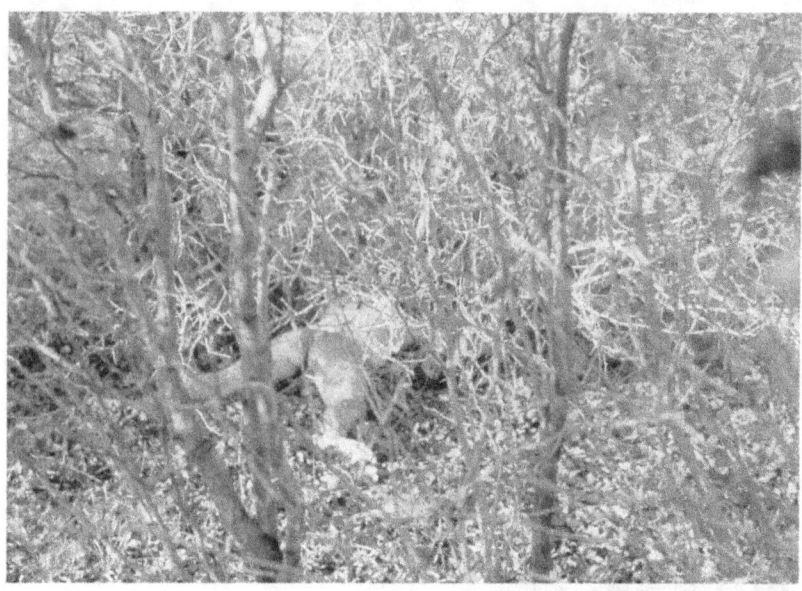

Plate 6. Ana Mendieta, *Rape Piece*, 1972. Color photograph documenting performance at the University of Iowa. Courtesy of the Estate of Ana Mendieta and Galerie Lelong, New York.

and femininity is derivative of masculinity.[28] Woman occupies a secondary place, liberation from which is, as Kuspit says of Mendieta, "liberation from sex." "One can regard Mendieta's performances as purification rituals," he writes, "bathing herself in the purity of the elements—once again innocently naked in nature—she becomes, emotionally, a sacred virgin, that is liberated from sex, untouchable by man."[29] Kuspit takes for granted that nature is innocent, virginal, and untouchable. He cannot imagine feminine desire or see the operative condition of desire in Mendieta's work except as that of the child/virgin.

This theoretical blind spot handicaps both male and female critics' understanding of Mendieta's engagement with nature. Given the long-standing associations between nature and the feminine, each is susceptible to sexist stereotypes. Just as it is inconceivable to Kuspit that Mendieta would desire to touch instead of to be touched, that her sexuality could exceed passivity, so it is impossible to imagine nature as desirous, sexual, and aggressive. Mendieta's earthworks have consequently been as misunderstood as her body art.

In 1969, ushering in the new decade, Cornell University's Andrew Dickson White Museum of Art organized what would be one of the most influential exhibitions of earth art in the United States. The exhibition catalog, written by Willoughby Sharp, claims that earth art, which began to appear in 1966, marks a formative break with modernism since it is "independent of the last dominant mode, minimal sculpture." Sharp attributes the break to the new materials, methods, and tools of these artists, along with their concern for the physical rather than the geometric properties of their media. In addition, he lists an intimate relation to the site, impermanence, antiobjecthood, subversion of style, focus on process, and lack of a pedestal as constitutive features of the new genre. Moreover, he notes what would later be recognized as earth art's postmodern aesthetics. "The new works," he writes, "seem to proclaim the artists' rejection of painting and previous sculptural concerns; the production of artifacts; the commercial art world and its consumer ethos; the urban environment; and the long-standing esthetic preoccupations with color, composition, illusion, and the internal relation of parts." Thomas Leavitt, the museum's director, proposes that earth art would do no less than the trumpets outside the walls of Jericho, claiming that "it is even conceivable that a new kind of museum, a true 'museum without walls,' could come into being."[30]

Mendieta's *Siluetas* are the inheritors of the legacy whose details the "Earth Art" show enumerated. Like the work exhibited there, they reject modernist conventions and advocate a restaging of the art experience. The series was, for the most part, executed in Iowa (where she lived) and Mexico (where she visited in the summer) before her move to New York City in 1978. In this series, she first used her own body and later a plywood cutout as its surrogate to mark her silhouette on dirt, grass, sand, mud, snow, or ice. She used both an additive process, molding her material in low relief on the earth's surface, and a subtractive process, carving through her natural materials to form a shallow depression.[31] Other variations on the *Silueta* theme employed the earth as a background against which to cluster flowers, berries, cloth, sticks, rocks, or shells in figural shapes. Mendieta carried the disappearance of the art object to its most extreme when she produced works in which she dug a narrow channel into the body of an earthen figure, poured gunpowder in the channel, and set it ablaze. Such pieces burned until only ashes remained.

While her work shares a great deal with that of the artists featured in the "Earth Art" show, hers diverges in its anthropomorphic and spiritual components as well as in its interrogation of the conventional meanings ascribed to nature. The dominant forms of earth art display a formal purity influenced by landscape architecture, geological excavation, building construction, agriculture, or astronomy. Sharp states unequivocally that, despite these disparate influences, all earth art shares "a total absence of anthropomorphism."[32]

In contrast, Mendieta's *Siluetas* were unmistakably human: they breathed fire and smoke, dripped blood, grew, disintegrated, and were reborn. In a 1977 interview, Mendieta said that "men artists working with nature have imposed themselves on it. Definitely my work has that feminine sensibility. I can't think of many men who would use a heart image in a serious way."[33] To anthropomorphize the earth is to endow it with sentience, desire, and identity; it is to think of earth as more than merely a sculptural material.

Mendieta's *Fetish* series, in which she molded bodies on the ground, moving from the flatness of the *Siluetas* to a more three-dimensional form, has specifically ritualistic connotations. The works in this series are marked with blood, branded with a branding iron, or pierced with sticks so as to suggest a "primitive" magical transformation. These works in particular were strongly influenced by Mendieta's knowledge of the rituals of Santería (an Afro-Cuban religious tradition), in which blood, hair, gunpowder, or candles are used to divine answers to specific questions or to bring about desired events.[34] With its pantheon of deities all of whom are associated with specific natural phenomena, such as rain or wind, Santería is pervasive throughout Mendieta's art. Her belief in a life force or "universal energy" that reverberates through all organisms, and in the ritual invocation of *ashé* or divine power, magically animated her works with anger, pleasure, hunger, and longing.

The elements of ritual and nature-centered theology prominent in the *Fetish* works were a synthesis of the investigations (by artists like Betsy Damon, Mary Beth Edelson, and Jane Ellen Gilmore) into goddess-centered spirituality, her own Cuban heritage, and the aesthetics of disappearance. The synthesis that Mendieta attempted in the *Fetish* series achieved its fullest expression in perhaps the best known of her sculptural works, the *Rupestrian Sculptures*, which she executed in the Escaleras de Jaruco outside Havana in 1981. She carved these relief figures in and around a large cave accessible only through dense jungle. The reliefs were inspired by her readings of Lydia Cabrera's books about the Taino (native Indians of Cuba). Mendieta invokes the Taino culture, religious beliefs, and language in the Taino words with which she titled the carvings.[35] Like the Taino, Mendieta's sculptures are destined to live and die with the earth to which they are connected.

While I will pursue the gender implications of her earthworks in subsequent chapters, it is important to note from the outset that Mendieta's work also provoked goddess spiritualism and troubled her female colleagues' undifferentiated notion of the feminine. In her recent reexamination of the trend, Gloria Feman Orenstein (an important early exponent of the movement) explains:

> In the seventies, women artists reclaiming the Goddess were looking for a unity beyond the pluralism of culturally specific symbols. It was important to them to learn that Goddesses once existed everywhere, and that their presence tended, on the whole, to give women higher status in their societies. At the time, feminists did not realize that this retrieval of a worldwide Goddess civilization was largely being done by white, middle-class women for the sake of what some have called an "essentialist" theory until it was pointed out to them.[36]

Although Mendieta was sympathetic with this movement's goals, she distanced herself from what she called "white feminism"[37] and the interests in the body, goddess culture, and the earth maintained by her white colleagues. Mendieta did express an interest in the earth as goddess, leading Orenstein, along with other writers such as Christine Poggi, Monica Sjöö, and Barbara Mor, to see her art as evidence of a growing trend among early second wave feminists to find empowerment in primordial female archetypes.[38] But what Orenstein and the other white critics overlook is the extent to which Mendieta's notion of the earth as goddess was culled from her knowledge of Santería and her readings about the beliefs of the Taino. Not recognizing the critical difference between their own and Mendieta's fascination with the earth, they appropriate Mendieta to a white goddess model and dis-locate her understanding of the earth from its origins in specific Cuban cultural traditions.[39] It is difficult not to read this dis-location as a "whitening" of the image of the earth goddess, as a way of purifying it of its roots in African and indigenous cultures.

Unfortunately, to locate Mendieta within Cuban culture may prove no easier than locating her within feminism. That she espoused a pro-Castro politics only increased her minority status within the already marginalized group of Latin American artists. In the catalog of the 1989 exhibition "Fuera de Cuba," for example, Mendieta is included, not for her art, but as the straw man of Communist brainwashing. Ileana Fuentes-Perez mentions Mendieta in an essay in which she claims that the Cuban government restricts information about artists exiled in the United States except for those like "Ana Mendieta, whose acceptance and official sponsorship in Cuba were tied to her open rejection of Cuban exile realities and her militance [sic] in pro-Castro circles, all of which served Cuba's propaganda quite well." [40]

Published in 1989, the same year as the fall of the Berlin Wall in Germany and in the midst of the decline of socialism in Eastern Europe, the "Fuera de Cuba" catalog bears the influence of a Cuban immigration process very different from the one Mendieta experienced in 1961. It comes at the end of the Reagan presidency, which itself had been ushered in with the 1980 Mariel boat lift, one of the final legacies of the Carter administration. During the Mariel exodus, some 120,000 Cubans emigrated to the United States from the port of Mariel after the Cuban government permitted unrestricted travel. The result of an unsuccessful series of tense negotiations between the two countries, Mariel was perceived by some as a means of revenge against the United States. Because such a huge number of refugees were unleashed on the U.S. immigration system, and because Castro allegedly forced criminals and mental patients to be included among those leaving, Mariel immigrants were not given the same economic and political support as those who came during the 1960s. [41]

The Mariel exodus was the impetus for Reagan's reestablishment of the travel ban to Cuba and a means for his administration to make Cuba "the focal point of [its] anti-communist crusade." During the Reagan presidency, Cuba was perceived as a direct threat to U.S. Central American policy; it was tied to conflicts in both El Salvador and Nicaragua. [42] As a result of the reintensification of the U.S. embargo, Cuba experienced greater economic and political isolation, and an acute financial crisis ensued. This was coupled with persistent accusations of human and civil rights abuses on the part of the Castro regime. The economic, political, and media war against Cuba by the United States seemed to result in Cuba's more extensive and violent control of its citizens' freedom. Cuba's increasingly dictatorial structure is the subject of Fuentes-Perez's essay (and more generally the catalog of which it is part). She suggests that exiled Cuban artists are the victims of Castro's restrictive policies, which forced them to escape the paralyzingly censorial Ministry of Culture.

The experience of more recent exiles, coupled with a growing Cuban American political constituency in U.S. politics, made Ana Mendieta's view of Cuba seem anachronistic. Unlike many of the artists mentioned in the catalog, she had left Cuba only two years after the revolution while its humanistic and nationalistic goals still seemed clear and admirable. [43] She did not experience what Fuentes-Perez describes as Marxist indoctrination, social isolation, or arrest.[44] She had come, not on a crudely and hurriedly constructed raft, but in an airplane. She had been allowed to travel to Cuba in the early 1980s, a privilege that seemed suspicious to Mariel exiles, for whom the travel ban was reinstated.

It should be sufficiently obvious at this point that mapping Ana Mendieta's relation to the art and politics of the 1970s and 1980s is an enormously difficult task. While she participated in and was influenced by body art, performance, earthworks, women's liberation, and Cuban politics, she is often excluded from their sometimes overlapping terrains. Although she frequently appears in exhibitions and texts that attempt to chart the unknown territories of performativity, femininity, and Latinity, she is just as often absent from them, for good and for bad. Mapping the margins may serve only to reinforce the centers and, ultimately, the power of those who occupy them.

This is a danger against which artist Luis Camnitzer warns in his discussion of Mendieta. Camnitzer recognizes the problematics of placing her too easily within a modern (Western) aesthetic tradition and suggests that her work is both shaped by and resistant to such classification: "Her work was often seen as a programmatic expression of feminism enhanced by a U.S. perception of mysterious exoticism. It was therefore also seen in the context of the superficial anthropologism prevalent in art. Some of her successes within these perspectives can be attributed to misunderstanding. Her work is not programmatic. It is, much more simply and modestly, a self-portrait."[45] Camnitzer is quite right to critique the ways in which critics tend typically to write about Ana Mendieta. As a female artist of the mid-1970s and early 1980s whose work was most prominently exhibited at feminist galleries like A.I.R. and the Women's Building or in group shows whose focus was on Latin America, Mendieta is usually categorized either as a *feminist* or as ethnically *other*. As a result of the curatorial need to make connections between works of art rather than to expose differences, few historians ask, How is Mendieta's feminism different from that of the other women with whom her works are exhibited? Does her work have significance outside the marginalized realm of Latinidad?

At the same time that Camnitzer forces some distance between Mendieta's work and dominant art-world interpretations, he also ironically comes to the same conclusions: Mendieta's art is not "programmatic" (by which I take him to mean "political"); it is "modest"; it is a "self-portrait." Camnitzer is more sensitive to the particularities of Mendieta's ethnicity than Orenstein is, for instance, but he remains insensitive to the feminized terms in which Mendieta's art is usually cast. To say that her works (which quite often burned, bled, or exploded) are "modest" is practically to suggest that they blush.

Camnitzer has commented that "the dual perception of her work as ethnic and feminist separated [Mendieta] two steps from the art of the U.S. mainstream."[46] Although the feminist and ethnic labels are to some extent useful, they are often a means by which critics or their audiences can distance themselves from the more important and perhaps threatening implications of her work. The reductive quality of these labels helps produce superficial interpretations resembling contemporary advertising. The work's perceived personal significance ("it helped her heal the wounds of her exile"), gender significance ("it's about the experience of woman"), and ethnic significance ("it's about being a Latina") are turned into memorable slogans. Such characterizations isolate her work to a specialized demographic and may occlude its relevance to broader questions of identity and nationhood. Camnitzer's own attempts to escape the labels under which Mendieta's work suffers backfire: he reverts to an apolitical stance, suggesting that her work is primarily a matter of a self-portrait. He tries to empty her work of the identity politics that nonetheless exceeds his critical vision.

The numerous attempts to control and contain Mendieta as well as the resilient excess of her work make it all the more necessary to clear a space for her—a space in which to think about the relation between her work and significant social, aesthetic, and political issues. At the same time, it would be unconscionable to think that this space might efface the emotionally and personally charged implications of the work. To eschew the personal in order to demonstrate a "broader" significance for a body of work is to maintain the false dichotomy of public versus private, or personal versus political, on which such marginalization depends. Mendieta's work in particular demonstrates the inviability of this dichotomy and requires an approach that does not valorize one category at the expense of another but rather undermines the coherence of the categories and their presumed mutual exclusivity.

Unfortunately, the problems do not end there. Even if one is able to satisfy those competing demands, the problem of history remains. Mendieta's identity strains historiography to the extent that it threatens to obviate the very practice of art history. Through their media, audience, influences, and themes, the works (like other time arts of the period) have persistently eluded and problematized a coherent discourse in the history of art since the 1970s. They require a major rethinking of the historiographic methods by which they are analyzed, largely as a result of internal, ontological contradictions.

As earthworks that existed in remote sites for limited periods of time, whose creation may have been witnessed only by Mendieta or a small group of guests, their audience is limited. The designation *performance art* may have slightly increased the numbers of those who witnessed Mendieta's acts of creation and burning. When these same acts were duplicated in photographs and films, they gained the wider audiences that belong to galleries and museums, articles, books, and catalogs. Yet few people have seen any of her works "in person." Few have seen her work "live," in the moment of its disappearance in time and space. The disappearance of the work is a serious limitation to writing about it, yet that sense of loss is central to its meaning.

The variety and immediacy of these pieces, along with their mediation through photographs and films, make them very hard to stabilize. They seem defiantly to tease us, preying on the limits of our vision, daring us to act on faith, forcing us to accept their disappearance. Few historians have been able to accommodate the mortality staged by such art. Even those who champion the experiments made by artists of this period, which question art's formalism and materialism, are perplexed by the contradiction that they mandate for the historian. Henry Sayre's enormously useful *The Object of Performance*, for example, wrestles with the question of how to preserve something the entire point of which is to question preservation, or, as I am using it here, *location*.[47] Until these theoretical problems are addressed, very little will be gained, and a good deal might be lost, by "locating" the 1970s or Mendieta's place in that decade's particular ferment.

PERFORMATIVITY, IDENTITY, AND EXILE

> The "coherence" and "continuity" of "the person" are not logical or analytic features of personhood, but, rather, socially instituted and maintained norms of intelligibility.
> —Judith Butler, *Gender Trouble*

What historiographic and theoretical paradigm is appropriate and helpful in understanding Ana Mendieta's work? Common assumptions about the nature of identity and the preciosity of the art object do not apply. I have found, to the contrary, that theories of performativity in fact underscore the very problem of writing about Mendieta at all. By *performativity* I do not mean to limit my analysis to those works that might be considered performance art in the strictest sense. Rather, I mean to call attention, first, to the aesthetic premises on which the work is based and, second, to the theoretical premises on which critical analysis of that work is based.

Focusing on the aesthetic premises of the work roughly corresponds to the approach that Henry Sayre takes to art produced since 1970. I will argue for Mendieta, as Sayre does for other artists, that, in general terms, all her works can be thought of as performance to the extent that they invoke disappearance, movement, and indeterminacy. In this way, her works fit into the trend toward "dematerialization" begun in the 1960s. They exemplify the category that Sayre calls the "other modernism": the modernism that refuses to fetishize the object in emphasizing contingency, fragmentation, and disembodiment.

While Sayre's analysis is extremely effective in accounting for the often-misunderstood aesthetic decisions of artists in this period, it offers not so much an alternative form of critical interpretation as a change in emphasis. I think that we need to go further to develop a critical language that can accommodate both the aesthetics of disappearance and the politics of identity and power that are central to these works. So focusing in turn on the theoretical premises of the work invokes *performativity* as it has been variously defined in the field of performance studies. For my purposes, *the performative* describes a special class of actions that are derived from and may be plotted within a grid of power relationships. Like the more common notion of performance, its emphasis on liminality over legibility and change over fixity is effective in placing interpretative emphasis on actions rather than on commodifiable objects. Yet it does not marginalize performance as a narrowly artistic endeavor but rather opens up artworks as social practice to the relations and interrelations—the performances of everyday life and culture—in which they are embedded. It goes beyond the idea of performance to consider in greater detail the conditions of identity, the practice of historiography, and the effects of representation and, indeed, thus, to encompass Mendieta's work.

Performativity expands, even breaks, the identity categories that have plagued Mendieta.[48] Performative identity is not homogeneous, stable, essential, and unified (and therefore limited to personality and/or ethnic type) but unfixed and destabilized in a way that makes its political imbrications paramount. In Judith Butler's analysis, which is influenced strongly by Derrida, performance is not acting but a repetition of (dis)-empowered acts.[49] It involves performing actions and utterances that are already heavily encoded semiotically, already imbued with power. She suggests that we think of identity, not as something that we have, but as something that we do. Identity is, for Butler, the effect of highly regulated action that nonetheless, as action, as process, necessarily erodes oppressive identity categories. She consequently helps us ask on Mendieta's behalf, "To what extent is 'identity' a normative ideal rather than a descriptive feature of experience?"[50] We have seen how merely describing Mendieta as a feminist or a Latina helps normatively secure her legibility, fix the location of her identity.

Just as Butler is suspicious of the presumed benefits of establishing identity categories, Peggy Phelan is suspicious of the presumed benefits of political visibility for the subaltern. She argues that, in their rush to visibility, minorities and women become victim to their own public representations, which contribute to rather than subvert dominant ideologies. She reminds us that there is real power in remaining unseen politically. She privileges the strategic potential of performance as, in her terms, "representation without reproduction."[51] She argues for a kind of performance that, by its very nature, privileges disappearance and accepts blindness. Following Phelan, performativity is a powerful lens through which to see the Other as unseen, to imagine a place "outside" strictly defined identity categories, outside or at least on the tenuous edges of legibility.

Performative identities are not false; they are not the function of the kind of artifice or masking that implies a hidden "real" self; rather, they challenge the coherence of that presumed real. To say that Mendieta performed identity in her works is not to say that she acted (in a theatrical sense) an identity that was not always already hers or that she played a role that momentarily disguised her "real" self. In the performance of identity, and in identity as performance, Mendieta is and is not "herself." She negotiates among identity possibilities that themselves emerge with the act of performance. No one true identity exists prior to the act of performing. No one identity remains stable in and through performance. Understanding identity as having these "performative" qualities enables a discussion of gender, color, nation, and ethnicity that bypasses essentialist categories. It allows us to ask, "Where is Ana Mendieta?" (implying contingency), instead of, "Who is Ana Mendieta?" (implying an unconditional truth).

A performative paradigm or approach is also useful in negotiating the difficult question of the personal versus the political. Through Butler's work in particular, it is impossible to distinguish between specific "personal" acts and broader "political" acts and counter-acts. Performativity undermines the easy location of identity in part by undermining the coherence of categories like the personal and the political, by seeing individual acts as inseparable from complex discursive power relations.

Performativity configures the artist's work as something more than an object or a theatrical performance; it helps reinforce the claim that the work actually makes something happen. J. L. Austin carefully distinguishes his seminal definition of the performative from performance per se. While performance is, for Austin, acting or mimetically re-creating the real, the performative effects very real change. It constitutes reality. His often-quoted example "I take this woman to be my lawful wedded wife" does not merely describe but literally forms a legal bond.[52] In other words, as Derrida has explained, the performative "produces or transforms a situation, it effects."[53] I will claim that Mendieta's works are, likewise, profitably, considered not in terms of description or mimesis, but in terms of their ability to produce new homes for identity, new conditions of being and identifying. Not only is her work incompatible with established, hyperintelligible identity categories, but as such it is powerfully disruptive to those categories.

Performance theory provides the means to make a series of claims about Mendieta's art that will form the main argument of this book. First, I will argue that Mendieta's imbrication of the body and the earth moves each into a reconsideration of *body* and *earth* that allows for their multivalent and overlapping significance. Just as the word *female* immediately invokes a paradigm of gender (in which an elaborate and extensive ideology of bodies and their identities comes into play while at the same time denying its own existence), so the word *earth* invokes a paradigm of place (in which ideologies of territory, indigenousness, and ecology take hold while being disguised as *nature*). Again, just as it seems impossible to use the word *female* without invoking the ideology of gender, so it is impossible to use the word *earth* without in part invoking the ideology of nation. It will therefore be my contention that, by engaging the earth as both material and theme, Mendieta's works engage theories of gender and nation in dialogue. They interrogate their respective and reciprocal statuses in (feminist) history.

In addition, I will argue that Mendieta's performative process of artistic creation is parallel to the performativity of the nation-space. While Judith Butler and other feminist critics have invoked theories of performance to frame gender politics, Homi Bhabha and other cultural critics have applied the framework of performativity to understanding the ideology of the nation. Under this paradigm, the nation is neither a thing nor a geographic location but the effect of especially narrative repetitions. Enactment brings the nation into existence on the performative power of "home," patriotism, government, and land.

With nationality comes exile. It is its mirror double. I consequently view exile, like the nation, as performatively produced. This is to say that *nationality* and *exile* are not descriptive terms but rather active conditions, the limits of which are created in performance. Like the nation, exile is more than a location (or, more precisely, a lack of location). It is a product of a set of meanings that both engage and undermine the narrative of the nation. As such, I imagine it as a liminal state with the power to subvert nationalist rhetoric. My eagerness to suggest a powerful function for a seemingly disempowered identity is the result of a spate of articles on Mendieta that view her exile only in terms of loss, sorrow, and personal trauma. In no way do I want to privilege exile as a utopian category, refusing to see its dire consequences. I am made cautious by Edward Said's admonition that "to think of exile as beneficial, as a spur to humanism or to creativity, is to belittle its mutilations." [54]

To this discussion I would add, however, that there is a difference between the advantages that I am ascribing to exile and those against which Said warns. I want to show how Mendieta herself occupied her exile as a discursive position from which to create her art, how she relied on its performativity (its accumulation and dissimulation of force, to use Butler's terms) to challenge presumed realities. Mendieta performs her exile broadly so as to interrogate nationality, color, ethnicity, and gender. Exile, here, refers not so much to her lived experience of national displacement as to a staged identity to which we become witness. Exile is itself the perfect answer to the question with which I began. Where is Ana Mendieta? To say that she is in exile is both to answer the question and to render it unanswerable.

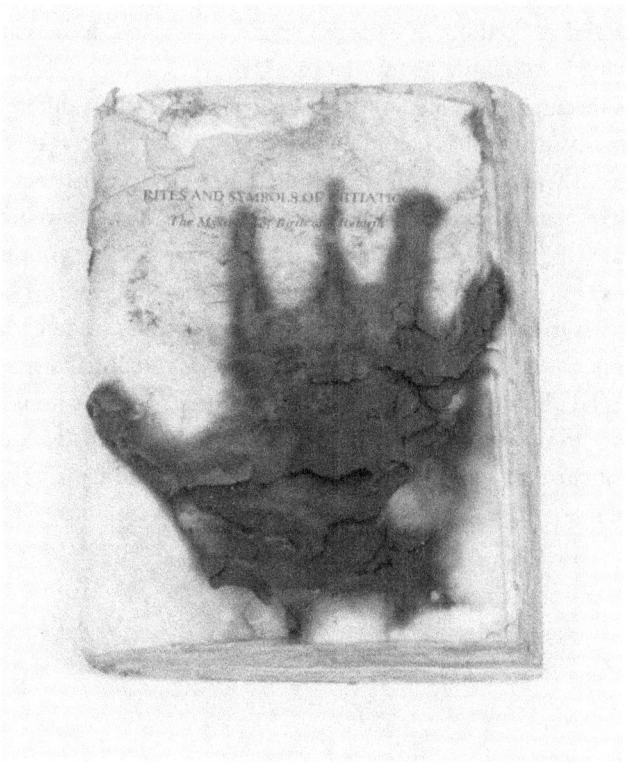

Plate 7. Ana Mendieta, untitled, ca. 1978. Branded handprint on book titled *Rites and Symbols of Initiation: The Mysteries of Birth and Rebirth.* Courtesy of the Estate of Ana Mendieta and Galerie Lelong, New York.

Chapter 1

FIRE

All these cinders, he feels them burning his flesh. —Jacques Derrida, *Cinders*

In 1978, Ana Mendieta burned the title page of Mircea Eliade's *Rites and Symbols of Initiation* with a branding iron formed in the shape of her own hand (pl. 7).[1] The burn goes deep; the first five or six pages are reduced to feathery black ashes where the palm of the iron hand pressed down hard. The imprint of the fingers appears more slender, and its touch is less harsh, but it has scorched a few of the title's black letters. The cover of the book has been torn from the binding to reveal the vulnerable white leaves that are now warped and curled at the corners. The smoke from the fire has defiled the leaves; they appear dirty, battered, and fragile. It is hard to get through the density of meanings encoded in this gesture of branding. A brand is meant to claim ownership, to stigmatize, or to signify the contents of a vessel. It disintegrates like words, burns and yet loses its hold like names. It is a self-effacing mark, Derrida's cinder.

I begin here with fire, with ashes, with words on the printed page, because in them I see Ana Mendieta's methodology, her performative practice of marking through disappearance. That dissolutive practice is absolutely central to the interpretation of her oeuvre. It is important both because it was employed in varying degrees by an entire generation of artists and because it relates directly to the themes with which Mendieta engaged. One of the four essentials, fire is as evanescent as speech, as elusive as certainty, as animate and unstable as identity. I see Mendieta's branding of Eliade's book as paradigmatic of her engagement with the contradictions of gender, ethnicity, and nationality; I want to finger the book's pages to see how she plays with fire.

Identity's politics is naming, a necessary practice inflamed by an underlying belief in innate qualities, by the presumption of authenticity or of essences that flicker and burn. The period of Ana Mendieta's active career coincides directly with the era of both divisive feminist arguments around the issue of essentialism and radical subaltern critiques of identity. These incendiary debates, whose flames were fanned throughout the 1970s, 1980s, and early 1990s by the winds of Marxism, women's liberation, poststructuralism, deconstruction, postcolonialism, and psychoanalysis, have proved difficult to contain.

Even if we momentarily (and artificially) isolate the debate on essentialism and gender from other battles over the nature of identity, the issues become only slightly more manageable. One might state simplistically that, in the context of early second wave feminism, women artists like Judy Chicago, Harmony Hammond, Mary Beth Edelson, Hannah Wilke, and Buffie Johnson formed a collective political response to sexism through a celebration of and insistence on the innate qualities of femininity and the notion of a recognizable feminine aesthetic. Their efforts have been reinforced by such theorists as Luce Irigaray, Hélène Cixous, Silvia Bovenschen, and Tania Modleski. Poststructuralism and identity politics, on the other hand, have drawn attention to the differences among women and to the classist, racist, and homophobic tendencies that have remained hidden (although some would say hidden in plain view) within feminism. As a result, many women artists turned against the universalism of feminism's essentialist philosophy. One thinks of Laurie Anderson's cyborg performances, Catherine Opie's photographs of lesbians costumed as men, or Mary Kelly's investigations into the psychoanalysis of gender construction. Their critiques of the essential category *woman* have been buttressed by the work of Toril Moi, Judith Butler, Eve Sedgwick, and Elizabeth Spelman.

The debate as I have sketched it here is, however, only a schematic for a much more intricate relation of discourses that only proliferate more questions. If gender is constructed, then how, and by whom? Is gender/sex determined by culture or chosen freely by the individual? Is gender the constructed half of the sex/gender binary; in which case, is sex really free of social inscription? Does the problem lie with the body and our conception of it or rather with the phallogocentric language and epistemology through which we are forced to see it? What is the real, concrete effect of either essentialism or antiessentialism as political practice? How do these issues play out in relation to identity categories beyond and in combination with gender? What historical and political influences have prompted the varying responses to the question of essentialism, and why is it being asked now?

It is well beyond the scope of this project to attempt a detailed and accurate summary of all the theoretical and artistic responses to these questions. My point is rather that feminists on all sides of the debate are burned by the contradictions mandated by the epistemology of identity, a fact made evident by at least two important books on the subject: Diana Fuss's *Essentially Speaking* (1989) and Naomi Schor and Elizabeth Weed's more recent anthology *The Essential Difference* (1994).[2] These books testify to the insolubility of the essentialist/constructionist debate. They take up Simone de Beauvoir's question, "What is a woman?" while at the same time asking, along with Judith Butler, "What can be meant by 'identity'?" Like Butler, they wonder "what grounds the presumption that identities are self-identical, persisting through time as the same, unified and internally coherent?"[3] But they are also suspicious of the political disengagement that can result from the strict application of Butler's deconstructive method. So they ask, to paraphrase Schor, to what extent does antiessentialism "secure feminism's place in male theory and recognition by it, notably the dominant male theory of the era, poststructuralism, which is most often to say, deconstruction?" To what extent is antiessentialism "the wages of academic legitimation?"[4] The possibilities for a resolution, a laying to rest of the problem, are limited only to a concession that essence and antiessence are inextricable. Even Judith Butler concedes that it is impossible to do away with identity categories and the dangers of essence that they imply.[5]

If we make room in our examination of identity for race, ethnicity, and nationality, the questions multiply exponentially. The radical examination of identity politics in the United States grew out of the civil rights movement, protests against the Vietnam War, and the advent of postcolonialism, each of which prompted a critique of dominant epistemologies of culture and identity. It was aided in the art world by the prolific (although often short-lived) formation of various ethnic, racial, and political groups throughout the 1960s and 1970s, such as the Art Workers Coalition, the Black Emergency Cultural Coalition, and El Movimiento Artistico Chicano. The Task Force on Discrimination against Women and Minority Artists, a group in which Mendieta was actively engaged in the late 1970s, was formed out of the same impulse. In addition, the critique of identity has been taken up by a huge and diverse group of writers, including Trinh Minh-ha, Gayatri Spivak, Cornel West, Gloria Anzaldúa, Homi Bhabha, Richard Dyer, and Kobena Mercer.

Following the debates around essentialism and antiessentialism and feminism, the insoluble problem for theorists of race, ethnicity, and culture lies in the contradictory benefits and dangers of identification. While Cornel West, for example, argues for the need to make vigorous claims on black identity, Trinh Minh-ha sees identity and authenticity as a trap. "I fear and reprove classification," she writes, "and the death it entails."[6] Are race and ethnicity biologically determined or culturally constructed? Does the claim that they are essential add to or detract from the power of racism? Does the claim that they are constructed disallow effective coalition politics? Is it possible to discuss race at all within dominant discourses and epistemologies? To what extent are these questions prompted by the commodification of diversity and the fashion for the multicultural?

Ana Mendieta's work encourages me to believe that, while gender, ethnicity, race, and nationality are offered as though one were free to take either an essentialist or a constructionist position relative to them, they are in fact constituted a priori by both philosophies. There is no freedom here. In order for them to exist as categories at all means that each must represent both an individual and a group, both difference and sameness. I agree with Judith Butler's claim that "naming is at once the setting of a boundary, and also the repeated inculcation of a norm."[7] At the same time, I want to insist, following Mendieta's example, that the boundary is made of ashes, that naming is as ambivalent and self-destructive as any other form of language subject to the surplus of meaning. "In a cinder of words," Derrida writes, "in the cinder of a name, the cinder itself, the literal—that which he loves—has disappeared." The name is ontologically a cinder because, the instant a name is used, it stands in place of, obliterates, burns the real, whose identity it is called to witness. Derrida's prose beautifully represents the combustion of the body by the name, essence by identity. He returns us once again to the charred remains of Eliade's book: "The urn of language is so fragile. It crumbles and immediately you blow into the dust of words which are the cinder itself. And if you entrust it to paper, it is all the better to inflame you with, my dear, you will eat yourself up immediately." [8] How is it, then, that the dry leaves of Eliade's text serve as kindling for Mendieta's fire?

Mendieta's art bears the imprint of feminism's most fundamental conflict, which was waged all around her throughout her career, yet the stakes were higher for her than for some women because femininity was the least of her problems. It was her most readily legible quality within the unyielding terms of identity; her ethnicity and nationality were far less clear. Mendieta did not solve this conflict in any definitive way. Rather, she brought to it an approach that revealed the instability of the footings on which it is built, an approach that conveys meaning through disappearance, makes marks with ashes, and draws our attention to a quivering flame.

This is a decidedly postmodern approach, one that would become the hallmark of a generation of artists who apply the 1960s notion of dematerialization to the critique of subjectivity, authority, identity, and history. What Mendieta shares with Guillermo Gomez-Peña, Glen Ligon, Yolanda Lopez, Cindy Sherman, Felix Gonzales-Torres, and any number of other artists coming to prominence in the 1970s and 1980s is neither medium nor necessarily subject matter but the method by which they engage in cultural critique. Sherman's staged self-portraits, for example, pile layers of femininity like petticoats on her absent "self" so that the photograph clicks on disappearance. Felix Gonzales-Torres's series of untitled candy portraits similarly invoke absence. These colorfully cellophane-wrapped piles of candy are meant to be taken, piece by piece, by an audience that literally consumes the work of art. Unlike traditional portraiture, which attempts to fix some inner identity to which the uniquely gifted artist is privy, Gonzales-Torres's works engage a sense of identity that is tenuous, unstable, and impermanent, realized in dispersal.

Mendieta may be said to apply the strategy of disappearance more literally than artists like Sherman or Gonzales-Torres do. Rebecca Schneider attempts to capture the unique quality of Mendieta's work by writing that, in it, "loss is not an anxious flirtation, not riddled with desire, displacement, or dislocation. Loss is present—literal, exigent, palpable." [9] Miwon Kwon asks (regarding essentialism and antiessentialism), "Might a reconsideration of Mendieta's work complicate the terms of the current feminist debate?" She answers that question by proposing that there is something enigmatic about Mendieta's art, "a peculiarity that spills over and exceeds this feminist framing. Mendieta's use of her/the body almost always approached erasure or negation: her 'body' consistently disappeared." [10] For Kwon, this disappearance is reiterated and made more palpable by its photographic documentation, a special kind of representation that, like the souvenir, replaces the "original" in a way that produces desire. For me, it is a performative marking, a refusal to satisfy the question at all, a means to trouble the very assumptions that enable it to be asked. Mendieta's work taken as a whole presents the female body but takes it back, reveals identity through disappearance, names by burning.

Ana Mendieta's use of identity categories plays between the one and the many, between essence and inessence. Rather than positioning herself on one side or another, she worked strategically with the inherent contradiction of the essential. In an often-quoted artist's statement, Mendieta explains:

> My art is grounded in the belief in one Universal Energy which runs through everything from insect to man, from man to spectre, from spectre to plant, from plant to galaxy.
>
> My works are the irrigation veins of the Universal fluid. Through them ascend the ancestral sap, the original beliefs, the primordial accumulations, the unconscious thoughts that animate the world.
>
> There is no original past to redeem; there is the void, the orphanhood, the unbaptized earth of the beginning, the time that from within the earth looks upon us. There is above all the search for origin. [11]

This statement is emblematic of Mendieta's strategy. At first glance, it seems irreducibly essentialist. To posit "one Universal Energy" and the search for origins is to rely heavily on a belief in essences and immutable properties. Yet she characterizes such properties as elusive, shifting, and subject to contradiction: "There is no original past to redeem. . . . There is above all the search for origin."

I am convinced that this contradiction owes its force to her fundamental conception of identity as orphanhood, as a loss of origin. Like Octavio Paz, by whose writing she was strongly influenced, Mendieta claims that identity, which is always approached only through the mechanism of separation and difference, is itself a form of exile. "All men," Paz explains, "are born disinherited and their true condition is orphanhood." [12] The exilic qualities of identity require that one is always tied to yet separated from those origins, groups, names, categories of existence, by which one is forced to define oneself. The paradox of essence is the paradox of identity; it is formed only through loss. There is no essence, only the search for essence; there is no identity, only the name; there is no origin, only the cinder.

Understanding how Mendieta successfully and at times problematically negotiated essentialism's minefield depends directly on one's recognition of the performativity of her work. As I stated in the introduction to this book, by *performative* I am referring, not to performance art per se, but to acts and utterances that, to paraphrase Butler, "put into effect the relation that they name."[13] When Mendieta refers to the "unbaptized" earth, she engages in and offers a specifically performative strategy for usurping the unyielding power of names.

To baptize is presumably to name through a "first act." It is to initiate a connection with civilization and religion, with both humanity and god. In the case of the earth, to baptize is to forge a relation with territory, nation, or agriculture. One imagines, for example, that Columbus "baptized" the earth of present-day Latin America by anointing it with the blood of the native and by claiming it in the name of Spain. Baptism, it should be noted, is the perfect example of Austin's performative in that the utterance of a few words transforms the identity of the baptized. To unbaptize is to place the initiate outside the name's reach. To unbaptize the earth is to unmark it, that is, to make it disappear from the binary structures that normally mark it as feminine, primitive, or undeveloped in a pejorative sense. It is a deconstructionist move that undoes the very hierarchies by which naming is organized. To unbaptize is to reveal the name as a cinder.

This strategy is everywhere in evidence in Mendieta's branded book. This work, it should be noted, stages an intense ambivalence in that it both relies on and questions Eliade's theories. I will argue that the work marks (in Phelan's sense) Eliade's text in such a way as both to interrogate its presumed authority and to redesign its construction of the primitive. The categorical distinction that Eliade sets up between primitive and modern ultimately reflects the presumed opposition between essentialist and constructionist philosophies, respectively. Mendieta's work exposes the binaries that Eliade erects between traditional man and modern man, between prehistory and history, between essence and inessence. In so doing, it shows the limitations of Eliade's legitimating historical view and, alternatively, finds power in unbaptizing origins.

Mendieta chose to brand a book, this specific book. By invocation and negation, she incorporates its discourses into her work. It is therefore necessary that we understand something of what that book is about.

Eliade begins *Rites and Symbols*, published in 1958, with an introduction that claims to differentiate types of thought, history, and epistemological conceptions of time in "modern" and "traditional" societies. He proposes to write a historical account that begins with a bit of musing about the conception of history in different cultures. In this regard, the text builds on his 1954 *The Myth of the Eternal Return; or, Cosmos and History*, which Eliade considered his most "significant" book, and which he recommended to new students of his work. In both texts, he places at odds two categories the defining qualities of which uncomfortably overlap: modern man and traditional man. In the 1954 book, he claims: "The chief difference between the man of the archaic and traditional societies and the man of the modern societies with their strong imprint of Judeo-Christianity lies in the fact that the former feels himself indissolubly connected with the Cosmos and the cosmic rhythms, whereas the latter insists that he is connected only with History." [14] Eliade's distinction between cosmos and history is parallel to that between essentialism and antiessentialism. The primitive believes in origins that confer power on all subsequent manifestations, whereas the modern believes in the accumulation of historical events directed by men. The essence is a kind of "beginning" through which cultural meanings are produced.

Mendieta upholds this division in her depiction of the primitive. Although contemporary individuals are far removed from their origins in the earth, she contends, the practices of "primitive" cultures signify their more direct relation to it. "It was perhaps during my childhood in Cuba," she writes, "that I first became fascinated by primitive art and cultures. It seems as if these cultures are provided with an inner knowledge, a closeness to natural resources. And it is this knowledge which gives reality to the images they have created." [15] Eliade utilizes the same idea four years after *The Myth of the Eternal Return* in *Rites and Symbols of Initiation* when he concludes that modern man is a fundamentally historical being but that traditional man tends "to project every new acquisition into the primordial Time, to telescope all events in the same atemporal horizon of the mythical beginnings." [16]

For Eliade, what distinguishes modern from primitive is not customs, languages, or relative levels of technological development but differing philosophies of history or, more accurately, the presence or absence of such a philosophy. First, he conceives of two different time systems, one that is primordial and endlessly repeatable through ritual, one that is linear and made up of unique and irretrievable acts. "Through the paradox of rite," he explains, "every consecrated space coincides with the center of the world, just as the time of any ritual coincides with the mythical time of the 'beginning.' "[17] Thus, for the primitive, every sacred act is a reenactment of one that took place before history, and, as such, each is in a sense a performative denial of history. For our purposes, this suggests that Eliade conceived of the primitive philosophy as essentialist: every identity is a reincarnation of the original identity; every woman, for example, is the enactment of Woman.

Mendieta's references to "ancestral sap," "original beliefs," and "primordial accumulations" seem to support this distinction. Like Eliade, she identifies prehistory with "primitive" or "traditional" man and history with the rights and obligations of contemporary life. Mendieta says only that primitive man is "closer to reality," but Eliade (in the book that she branded) provides specific examples from a wide variety of cultures around the globe of traditional man and his lack of a historical worldview. He takes examples from a broad range of initiatory rituals, including rites of pubescence, marriage, creation, and rebirth or resurrection. Common to all is the notion that what is being enacted in the ritual is directly related to a primordial prototype. He writes, for example: "It is impossible to exaggerate the importance of this obsession with beginnings, which, in sum, is the obsession with the absolute beginning, the cosmogony. For a thing to be well done, it must be done as it was done the first time." [18]

Significant here is Eliade's view, echoed by Mendieta, that traditional man is more concerned with the eternal — the continued presence of the first time — than with the temporal. He claims that all forms of initiation relate to the idea of death and rebirth and that rituals of this type actively seek to thwart death, time, and history. He describes one such ritual in which "the idea of gestation and childbirth is expressed by a series of homologizable images — entrance into the womb of the Great Mother (Mother Earth), or into the body of a sea monster, or of a wild beast, or even a domestic animal." [19] This statement has obvious resonance with much of Mendieta's work, including her First Silueta, which deals with themes of death and rebirth staged in an earthen, womb-like cavity (pl. 8). Here, the category woman is sanctioned by the first woman, by Mother Earth, by the biology of childbirth.

That she would have been interested in reading Rites and Symbols is indicated by the fact that passages like the one mentioned above seem to resonate with themes in her art. Most obvious is the belief, which Eliade assigns to the primitive, in the transcendence of human death through the

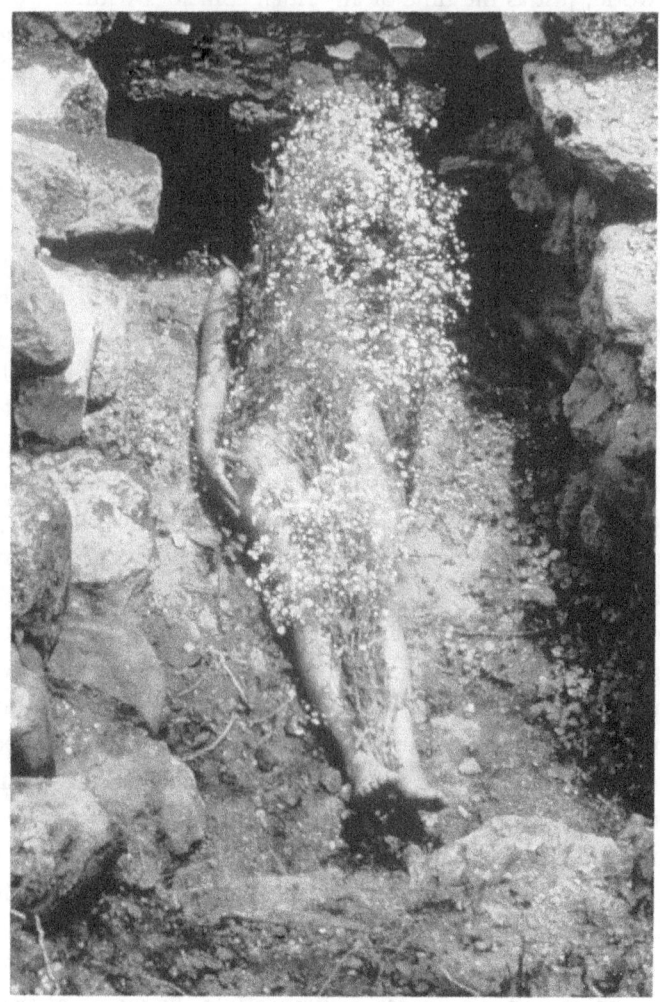

Plate 8. Ana Mendieta, *First Silueta*, 1973. Color photograph of earth/body work with flowers, executed at El Yaagul, Oaxaca, Mexico. Courtesy of the Estate of Ana Mendieta and Galerie Lelong, New York.

immortality of the earth or nature generally. In addition, Eliade writes, for example, about the sacrality of the earth in initiation rites, the pervasiveness of the belief in the symbolic power of blood, and the transformative effects of ritual.[20] More dramatic in the context of this work are those passages concerning the mystical significance of fire, which directly resonates with Mendieta's performance of branding. For example, Eliade reports that "many primitives think of the magicoreligious power as 'burning,' and express it in terms meaning heat, burn, very hot. . . . In addition, shamans are held to be 'masters over fire.' "[21]

Mendieta marks this text as if appropriating it, as if claiming it for her own. Her act is reminiscent of the "primitive" acts that the book describes; it could be the trace of some initiatory ritual, the sign of a crude, spontaneous reenactment of some primordial event, or an expression of what Mendieta takes to be her own "magicoreligious power." Seen in this way, Mendieta herself takes on the role of the "traditional man" whom Eliade's book recounts. Her performance reinforces Eliade's basic claims about the nature and importance of ritual in "primitive" societies while at the same time amending them slightly to demonstrate that initiatory ritual is not lost after all, that it is possible to revive its power in contemporary life. In this sense, Mendieta's branding may be read as simply a kind of visual affirmation of a text that she admired, suggesting that the meaning of the whole may be found between the pages of Eliade's book. Here, we have arrived at a perfunctory end to the process of interpretation. Her ideas about the "primitive" world repeat Eliade's to the extent that her performance of this ritual burning gains its efficacy as a repetition of the origin-affirming rituals that Eliade's book describes—except that Mendieta has still come close to incinerating this book.

In its conflation of cultures around the globe into one undifferentiated picture of "primitive" life, and in its exoticization of Third World cultures, which Eliade presents as romantically possessing what contemporary civilization has lost, Eliade's book is a problematic artifact in Mendieta's performance. It places these cultures on a developmental spectrum in which there is no "going back" to the primitive life, which Eliade has secured safely in a mythic past. Yet Eliade does not take for his object of study ancient cultures made extinct by colonial exploitation. Rather, he examines living cultures of Africa, the Pacific Islands, and remote areas of Latin America.

That he both bemoans and guards his First World privilege makes his perspective similar to that of the neocolonial whom Mendieta calls into question in her notes:

The colonization of the Americas in which the natural inhabitants where [sic] submitted to a violent system of inhuman exploitation which cost the lives of thousands of them including the extinction of whole cultures and people (i.e.: the Antilles) are [sic] evidence of this type of colonization. In the xx century however its [sic] incorporated a new type of colonization. No longer will open brutal violence be implemented. Colonization and neo-colonization will be disguised by modern tecnics [sic], to paraphrase the leading ideologists from the great colonizing Potencies: "to elevate the underdeveloped people to a higher standard of living." In the past as well as in our own century in order to facilitate the expropriation of the natural richness of a territory and/or use the people as labor, the process which has been and still is very much implemented is DECULTURATION. Its purpose being to uproot the culture of the people to be exploited.[22]

This passage reveals a great deal about Mendieta's investment in the issue of primitivism. First, it shows her sense of bereavement over the loss of entire civilizations at the hands of colonials, particularly in the Antilles. Second, it suggests that she perceived a similar pattern of exploitation to have developed in the twentieth century in those same regions. What was genocide in the fifteenth through the nineteenth centuries becomes deculturation in the twentieth. Finally, it demonstrates that Mendieta's interest in the native cultures of the Caribbean grew, not only out of anthropological curiosity, but also out of a strong sense of affinity with their experience of exploitation. In them, she saw herself, transplanted, exploited by political systems beyond her control, subjugated to the laws of others, robbed of her land, and separated from her culture. In Mendieta's view of the "primitive," she always to a certain degree sees herself. How can she both use Eliade's book and identify herself as a member of the Third World, which Eliade's ideology of development mocks?

Unlike Mendieta, Eliade does not celebrate what he describes as the primitive notion of time, the emphasis on the eternal, or the ritual re-enactment of cosmic prototypes. Rather, he takes pride in his "objective" presentation of the benefits and limitations of primitivist and modernist philosophies. In *The Myth of the Eternal Return*, Eliade polarizes primitive man and historical man, summarizing the paradigmatic elements of the essentialist/constructionist debate.

The constructionist (modern man) sees no origins that are free of history, no essence that is not constructed. He considers himself to be more liberated to create his own identity than primitive man, who is bound to primordial prototypes. He also considers primitive man to be in denial of what is manifestly true, that is, the inherent temporality and finitude of life and the consequent verity of a historical view of time. Eliade suggests that modern man accepts the mortality of humanity because of his unwavering belief in individual freedom. Modern man asserts his freedom to act independently, to make new histories that will be laid in series with countless others. In so doing, he relinquishes the belief in a prehistory.[23] For modern man, identity is determined by the freedom of the individual and the will to produce a distinct self. While contemporary constructionists are far more reserved about the nature and extent of freedom entailed in the social construction of identity, one of the political advantages of a constructionist perspective remains its implications for change. For Butler, for instance, we work both with and against the history of names: although identity is not a matter of will or free choice, neither are we solely at its mercy. It can be brushed against the grain. In Eliade's account, however, the misguided primitive trades his individual desire for the unthinking acceptance of prototypes, in repetitions of the same.

At the same time, the essentialist (primitive man) believes himself to be more free than his modern counterpart because, by returning to his origins, he effectively annuls the debilitating history created by man. He believes that modern man's freedom and power to create history is limited to a privileged few, who impose their creation on others through intimidation.[24] While contemporary essentialism is undeniably a product of a "modern" philosophy and therefore bears its debt to historicism, it retains the trace of this so-called primitive belief in that it seeks refuge from a history that seems intolerably repressive. It tries to transcend hegemonic cultural constructions by returning to powerful essences.

By building his argument on the scaffold of the essence/antiessence binary, Eliade falls into the contradictions at its core. Eliade's critique of traditional cultures' conception of time and history betrays a certain nostalgia for this conception, which, he argues, modern society has almost totally obliterated. It is not surprising that Eliade identifies himself with "modern man" and the burdens of modern consciousness: having a greater awareness of the "real" process of history than his "primitive" counterpart and yet, by his very wisdom and experience (which mark him as a member of an "advanced" culture), feeling a great sense of loss for the rituals about which he writes. Eliade laments in 1958 that "in the modern Western world significant initiation is practically nonexistent." In his earlier book, he states more pointedly that "the terror of history becomes more and more intolerable from the viewpoints afforded by the various historicistic philosophies."[25] Like Mendieta, Eliade's understanding of history produces a paradox in which the search for origins exists "above all" even though "there is no original past to redeem."

Mendieta's branding is an intensely ambivalent scar burned into the flesh of Eliade's book. It is a reminder of the pain involved in searching for origins. It is a mark that makes legible the shifting nature of that unattainable truth. The burned handprint challenges Eliade's claim that "what radically differentiates [traditional societies] from modern society is the absence of historical consciousness in them."[26] Here, the relation between Mendieta's gesture and Eliade's history becomes muddled—if Mendieta is performing a ritual act that, in Eliade's sense, is bereft of "historical consciousness," what are the implications of performing such a ritual with a prop that is itself notably historical? Mendieta's act (traced in the branded book) collapses the distinctions between cosmos and history, between essence and inessence, that Eliade so carefully maintains.

Yet the instability of these dichotomies makes Eliade's own hand tremble. He admits that "no such thing as an absolutely closed primitive society exists. We know of none that has not borrowed some cultural elements from outside; none that, as a result of these borrowings, has not changed at least some aspect of its institutions; none that, in short, has had no history."[27] Like the feminists writing twenty or more years later, Eliade recognizes that neither essences nor constructs exist independently of each other. He anticipates Diana Fuss's claim that "there is no essence to essentialism, that essence *as* irreducible has been *constructed* to be irreducible."[28] From the modern end of things, Eliade skates around other contradictions. He claims that history gains a foothold in the prospect of its own demise, in its complicity with a Judeo-Christian tradition in which "one tolerates history in the hope that it will end."[29] Keen to make his distinction between modern and traditional stick, he excises similarities between the Christian doctrine of resurrection and the "primitive" rituals of death and rebirth. In this, he falls prey to his own argument: he critiques the belief in the Beginning, the primary origin, while at the same time trying to place traditional societies at the beginning of his own history and, by doing so, to keep them pure, homogeneous, and untouched by historical change. By branding his book, Mendieta makes these contradictions visible: she plays between primitive and modern.

I do not mean to suggest that Mendieta had some uniquely privileged and clear view of the complexities and contradictions involved here. I do not believe that this work was self-consciously about all these issues; rather, essence and inessence, history and origins, modern and primitive, could not help but emerge as a product of Mendieta's own experiences and perhaps, more important, as a result of the internal instability of the terms of identity. Like Eliade, Mendieta found identity's paradoxes troubling; unlike him, she was victimized by them and learned in the most pragmatic way to dodge their blows.

The branded book is not a performance in the sense that it mimics a ritual act; Mendieta is not simply playing the role of the primitive. It is performative, however, to the extent that, in her branding, she not only relies on the accumulated force of the history of the "primitive" as a rhetorical category but also, to paraphrase Butler, "turns against this constitutive historicity." In her branding, she calls up the conventional representation of the primitive in order to burn it. She performatively marks the "universal," "ancestral," "primordial," and "original." In so doing, her performance produces a new teleology. She forges a link between the ritual performance and an imaginary prelapsarian moment from which it draws its strength. She legitimates it by seeming to repeat a ritual branding that carries the force of history, the weight of genesis, and the authority of essence.

Mendieta's corpus does suggest an "obsession with beginnings," with nature as the source of essentialism's power. Despite her attraction to nature's originary force, however, Mendieta was well aware that nature is unmarked, devalued, and rendered invisible in historical discourse. In its various incarnations as earth, female, and primitive, nature exists outside and in spite of the histories that uproot, ignore, and exploit it. It is slave to a powerful metaphysics that depends on its resources, its fertility, and its dependable labor. Mendieta also knew that simply adding the marginalized to the discourses of power does nothing to change those discourses, that, in fact, doing so often works to reinforce them. Making oneself visible may only legitimize the colonizing terms of visibility. In this sense, Mendieta understood Phelan's warning that "there is real power in remaining unmarked; and there are serious limitations to representation as a political goal."[30] By unbaptizing the earth, Mendieta separates it, and the female and primitive with which it is associated, from the assumption that visibility in history adds value or serves any beneficial purpose. Hers is a performance with a difference; hers is a marking that burns, and burning disappears. The following chapters take up this performance as it is enacted in other histories, other texts, and other fires.

Chapter 2

EARTH

I decided that for the images to have magic qualities I had to work directly with nature. I had to go to the source of life, to mother earth. — Ana Mendieta, in Sulfur

Ana Mendieta produced over two hundred works of art in which she used the earth as a sculptural medium. She molded it, burned it, and lay down on it. It was her source for rich artistic materials: wet sand, rock, gravel, mud, slurry, compost, soil, humus, peat, and clay. More than an inanimate object, the earth was a living process: at her hands it froze and melted, flooded and dried, eroded and deposited itself, fostered growth and decay. To say precisely what the earth meant to Mendieta—symbolically, emotionally, ideologically—is a much more complex matter. So ubiquitous is it in her art that one might begin to think of the earth as a stock character whose role is always the same. Yet this very ubiquity means that its signification should not be presumed. For Mendieta, the earth is neither simply the planet called *earth* nor simply the dirt beneath our feet. It is a womb, both sexual and maternal, the fundamental source of life, a homeland, a prehistoric origin, nation, nature, a landscape, a link to ancestry, a burial site, and a sentient being.

While these bountiful associations did not originate with her, her handling of them is much more than a simple reiteration. Much has changed in the retelling. In this chapter, I am proposing that, through its symbolic imbrication with the female, the earth is as culturally constructed, ideologically determined, and hegemonically controlled a concept as femininity itself. I will also urge that we excavate the meaning of *earth* to discover the seeds of nation buried within it. I want to imagine the implications of these connections for an artist who lived in exile and who played a significant role in advocating women's and minorities' rights. I will argue that Western mythologies secure the earth's white female personification—where femininity is understood to be maternal and where whiteness is presumed to be the norm. I will also claim that Mendieta conceived of the earth in Octavio Paz's terms as an origin (however unstable), an essence (however charred), through which subjectivity is constructed. This chapter, and to some degree the next, will take up the idea of the earth as a semiotic field uniquely suited to representing the process of identity formation.

When we say that Mendieta works with the earth, what precisely do we mean? How much distance lies between her earth and that of other artists working in the same medium? It is difficult to imagine, for example, that Mendieta's earth is the same as Alan Sonfist's when he describes the origins of the earth art movement in these remarkably jingoistic and colonialist terms:

> The artists' awareness of the Earth is growing worldwide, but the United States has become the center of artistic activities focusing on the idea. Art in the land is an American movement. The experimental atmosphere in the United States has led to the development of this innovative art within only a few years. In addition, it is significant that America still possesses great quantities of land to which artists have access. Land has always been a primary element in forging the American consciousness. One of the primary motives for coming to America was land. As long as there has been land, the direction of culture has been one of constant expansion.[1]

Even if Sonfist is attempting to suggest that earth art offers a unique opportunity to examine and interrogate America's troubling expansionism, he simultaneously proffers this art form as evidence of U.S. ascendency and dominance. Always the can-do innovator, he implies, America was the leader in "rediscovering" the earth as an artistic material. With its vast expanses of untamed land, America is, he suggests, nearly synonymous with the earth itself (a colonizing rhetoric if ever there was one). What could this mean to Ana Mendieta, an artist for whom *America* referred not only to the United States but to the entire Western Hemisphere, whose native country has long borne the violence of expansionism, and who was herself victimized by American (that is to say, U.S. and Central American) politics? Of course, there are different conceptions of earth at play in all the various incarnations that earth art has taken: Dennis Oppenheim's geometric constructions, Nancy Holt's astronomical structures, Robert Smithson's topographies, or Walter De Maria's meteorological experiments. What unites these artists, however, is a presumptive right to manipulate the land, a right of nationality established through birth, sanctioned by two centuries of American conquest, and memorialized in images from Thomas Cole to Ansel Adams. Ana Mendieta, an exile, could not expect the same privilege.

Central to her use of the earth are also the metaphoric associations that she draws between it and the female body. So ancient is this metaphor, so often has it been explored in the earth art movement, that it seems the most obvious of the earth's meanings. Mendieta's work has a strong affinity with that of Judy Chicago, Mary Beth Edelson, Betsy Damon, and Carolee Schneemann, all of whom explored the idea of the earth goddess as part of a distinctly feminist strategy. It is dangerous, however, to forge her connection to them, or their connections to each other, too eagerly. In reviewing Mendieta's work, Mira Schor, for example, sees in it only "generic" Venuses and woman "traditionally" understood as nature. She laments: "Mendieta's Woman, particularly in the later works, is only female, she presents a limited view of the form and experience of femininity out of the limitless possibilities of femaleness. Because dialogue and conflict do not flourish within a significant portion of her work, it does not have the depth of an oeuvre. In Mendieta's work there are many deeply moving and rivetingly memorable images, but, ultimately, the constant repetition of an unquestioned, generic (gyneric) Great Mother is deeply, and now, poignantly problematic." [2] Schor echoes a common perception that Mendieta's works are merely part of the now widely discredited goddess movement. In Miwon Kwon's words, they "veer strongly toward the essentialist pole in both intention and reception." [3] I remain unconvinced by this critique because it is predicated on notions of woman and earth that have yet to be examined. To whose traditions are we referring? Is the problem that Mendieta could not produce dialogue, conflict, or complexity in her image of woman or, rather, that we presume too quickly a familiarity with that image? Whom do we picture in our minds when we think of Woman? For what earth, what nature, does that Woman stand?

That Mendieta worked closely with the women's liberation movement, combining her efforts with those of artists such as Nancy Spero, Mary Miss, and Mary Beth Edelson to sustain the feminist gallery A.I.R. and to publish analyses of women's art and feminist issues in *Heresies*, is of enormous relevance to the feminine terms in which she cast the earth. But it should not be forgotten that she sometimes fought bitterly with these same women over the unfair treatment of minorities, specifically Latin Americans. In 1978, A.I.R. established the Task Force on Discrimination against Women and Minority Artists, a group with which Mendieta was heavily involved. In 1979, she participated in a program at the gallery on Latin American women artists that included Maria Lino, Liliana Porter, and Susana Torre.[4] And, in 1980, she organized the exhibition "Dialectics of Isolation: An Exhibition of Third World Women Artists of the U.S." Furthermore, as friend and film critic B. Ruby Rich has said: "She knew every Latin artist in New York, male and female, and was always pushing all of them—to be ambitious, to break the stereotypes, to make their mark. Ana's circle is the generation of feminist artists, Latino artists, black writers, feminist critics, unintimidated Cubans—a group of people who share more passion than power."[5] Given her nationality, ethnic identity, and political affiliations, Mendieta's philosophy of the earth must be understood differently than it often has been in the past.

Although critics have long discussed the role of gender and ethnicity in Mendieta's work, understanding these themes remains limited without a fuller accounting of nationality. That the bond between earth and nation has not been discussed relative to her art is hardly surprising since the earth is so often interpreted as the antithesis of nation. Earth is nature to the nation's culture. It is free from politics while the nation is defined politically, universal while the nation is particular, timeless while the nation is contingent. The invocation of earth, then, may seem to be a tacit disavowal of the nation. I am suggesting that Mendieta invokes the earth precisely because of its antithetical relation with the nation, precisely as a tool to combat its ideologies. This makes the nation integral to the earth's meaning and demands that their connection to each other be examined.

To the extent that earth and nation form a binary, each stands at the top of a lengthy list of related concepts. The earth is prehistorical, female, primitive, of the body; the nation is historical, male, colonial, of the mind. That is, the nation is the entity that (although at times invisible) gives meaning and urgency to those components forming Mendieta's conception of earth. *Earth* and *nation* also stand for two opposing philosophies of identity: the earth is essential, unified, and natural; the nation is constructed, multifarious, and artificial.

By invoking the earth, the essential, the female, the primitive, and the colonized, Mendieta appears to display, draw power from, and then disavow the ideas to which these notions are opposed. But I believe that she did more than simply validate the category *earth* (and all the notions that line up neatly behind it) and invalidate *nation*. Rather, by working with the conventions of the binary to represent identity but being unable herself to fit their regulatory practices, her work exposes their untenability.

In the previous chapter, I claimed that Mendieta managed essentialism's dangers through a performative method of unmarking or unbaptizing. This strategy was equally effective in the context of nationality since *nation* is itself constituted by the ambivalent play of essence and inessence. Like identity, the nation is, in Homi Bhabha's influential analysis, brought into being through performance. It is neither a material nor a conceptual entity; rather, it exists only in the repeated and stylized citation of words, actions, pledges, songs, images, symbols, and historic personages. It derives its performative force from what Butler calls "the citational legacy by which a contemporary 'act' emerges in the context of a chain of binding conventions."[6] Bhabha suggests that the performativity of the nation derives from the repetition of a specific ambivalent narrative, which he summarizes in the phrase "out of many, one." This, he claims, is the founding narrative of the nation. It is the central problematic of the nation as a structure, a structure that demands two contradictory things: on the one hand, in order to exercise hegemony, the nation must be conceived as a single entity, an essence; on the other, it must be conceived as a conglomeration of individuals, an enterprise of difference. This is nowhere made more clear than in the duality of the notion *the people*. Simultaneously this concept suggests a multiplicity of individuals and a monolithic entity.[7] Indeed, Bhabha argues that it is the very collectivity of the nation that creates, in a sense demands, individuals. The nation's ideal of an essential character cannot survive within the realm of "sameness"; it signifies only where essence can be located despite difference, a fact made evident by notions like the *melting pot* and *multiculturalism*. Out of many, one. For Bhabha, the essence of *one* is never achieved in any final sense because the one means nothing without the many. His analysis is another argument for dismantling the essence/antiessence binary. It demonstrates that the terms of the binary are not in fact oppositional but integral, indeed, synonymous. Therefore, the phrase "out of many, one" can stand, not only for the nation's contradictions, but also for those of other identity categories that presume to name both individuals and groups.

To consider how Mendieta negotiated the ambivalence of *nation*, to see how she both claimed and singed its texts, we must understand something about her specific experience of immigration, exile, and naturalization. Her perceptions of both Cuba and the United States were formed by each nation's multiple identities, the internal ruptures that lie underneath their external cohesion. She learned the meaning of *nation* by confronting not only the borders between the two countries but also those that crisscross within them. The Cuban revolution broke open the national identity of the island to reveal internal conflicts and divisions (between poor and rich, white and black, Communist and capitalist, city and country, men and women) that had lain partially buried after Cuba's revolution against Spain. When, on 6 April 1961, Fidel Castro declared Cuba a socialist country, he reopened the wounds of colonialism, rekindled the conflicts between landowners and farmers, between whites, blacks, and mulattoes, and revealed the nation as a decidedly deterministic rather than self-identical structure.[8] This declaration set off a series of events that would have pervasive consequences in Ana Mendieta's life.

In the days and years before Castro's announcement, the Mendieta family had been well known and highly regarded in Cuba. Mendieta's great-grandfather, Carlos Maria de Rojas, had been a general in the war of independence, and he became famous for an act of self-sacrifice in which he burned down his own sugar mill rather than allow it to benefit the Spanish government.[9] Mendieta's paternal grandfather had been a consul to Spain and a military leader, and her great-uncle Carlos Mendieta had been president of Cuba in the 1930s. Her father, Ignacio Mendieta, was a lawyer well connected to Cuban political leaders, and he aided in the 1959 revolution against Fulgencio Batista.[10] The Mendieta name was embedded within Cuban nationalism.

However, in 1960, evidence came to light indicating that Ignacio Mendieta had been trained by an FBI informant in the late 1940s as a counterintelligence agent and that, as a major in the National Police, he had pointed out suspected Cuban Communists. With Castro's announcement that his was a socialist revolution, and with the Cuban government's increasing economic and political ties to Communist countries, Ignacio Mendieta openly opposed him. Like many other Catholic Cubans, Mendieta viewed Castro's open admission of Communist affiliation as a threat to his religious and political beliefs. By defying his country's government, he became alienated from his patriotic lineage. He was sentenced to twenty years in jail for having aided the CIA in its Bay of Pigs invasion plans.[11] Ignacio Mendieta's long and brutal punishment is vivid evidence of the conflict between patriots and revolutionaries, between old and new national narratives.

In 1961, thousands of Cuban parents began sending their children to the United States through the help of U.S. corporate sponsorship, the charity of U.S. citizens, and the aid of the Catholic church. This exodus was a desperate response to Fidel Castro's plans to expand the socialization of Cuba and to the intensification of the U.S.-Cuban political conflict in the wake of the Bay of Pigs invasion. Ana Mendieta and her sister, Raquel, were the reluctant benefactors of this program, sent to the United States on 11 September 1961 in an airplane filled with other Cuban children.

With the cessation of U.S.-Cuban relations in January of that year, a rumor had circulated in both Cuba and Miami about Fidel Castro's plans to send Cuban children from their urban, upper-class homes out into the countryside to teach the peasantry.[12] Touted as a literacy program, the Education Ministry's plan seemed to have broader goals. It was a means of removing children from their positions of privilege in the cities (which in 1961 still bore the traces of the lavish lifestyles created by foreign investment) and sending them to the countryside, where they would "become more 'Cubanized.'" It was also a way of indoctrinating teenagers into Marxism and against capitalism. Finally, it was meant to isolate children from their parents so that they could be more easily instructed in the goals of the revolution and so that parents might be made to understand that allegiance went first to the state and second to the family. Artist Mario Bencomo recalls his experience of this policy: "I remember that in junior high school we were shown many documentaries and films, which our teacher then used as a source to teach us about the evils of capitalism. I was among several students chosen for a study scholarship to Czechoslovakia; I was thirteen when I was asked to sign a declaration vowing not to leave Cuba with my parents in the event they decided to do so."[13] The revolution tested the limits of the nation by encroaching on the territory and jurisdiction of the individual family, by redrawing the border between public and private. Mendieta's parents felt that it was better to send their daughters to the United States alone than to risk subjecting them to the kind of strict indoctrination and alienation from parental authority that the revolution promised.

The fear of Castro's program (the planning of which he denied) resulted in part from the significant economic disparities that had been highlighted by Cuba's conversion to socialism. The revolution itself was a response to the increasing gap between classes brought about by huge foreign investment in and profit from the Cuban economy (primarily by the United States). The contrast between the living standards of those in the cities and the living standards of those in the countryside was marked. In addition to the need for indoctrination, the Education Ministry's plan was intended to disrupt the class privilege of the urban children and turn their thoughts away from the attractive commodities provided by capitalist investment. Ana's cousin Raquel (Kaki) Mendieta explains the effect of this on the Mendieta family: "At that point began the contradictions typical of a Revolution. Class contradictions. Well, we came from a bourgeois family and we had to make a class jump, so to speak, we had to break away from a classist background, and incorporate ourselves into the revolution. Ana's family did not do it, and very quickly they drifted towards a position against the Revolution."[14] Not wanting to lose their class privilege or be made to associate with the lower classes (from whom they had been separated by centuries of tradition), many families, like the Mendietas, sought escape.

The girls' travel was made possible by the U.S. State Department's decision to grant visa waivers to "students" coming into the United States from Cuba; student was loosely defined as any child between six and sixteen years of age. Their trip was funded by a clandestine organization of U.S. businesses, such as Esso Standard Oil Company and Shell Oil, anxious to reclaim their property and assets in Cuba, which Castro's government had nationalized.[15] The organization through which donations were made to fund the children's flights to Miami became known as "Operation Pedro Pan."[16]

Once in the United States, the Mendieta girls became part of the troubled national identity of a country that was dealing with the baleful consequences of its own repressed colonial past. They arrived here at the height of the civil rights era and the beginning of the Vietnam War, a period of intense battles over racial purity, economic privilege, and mandatory patriotism. They were sent to live in Iowa, where there were few if any people of color, let alone other Cubans. There they were shuttled between foster homes, orphanages, and juvenile correction facilities. In her nomadic journey through the social welfare system run by Catholic Charities, and in her contacts with other children and teenagers, Mendieta's perception of herself changed dramatically. Having come from a prominent Cuban family that traced its heritage to Spain, the girls had never had to question their race or ethnicity; as Raquel has said, "it never entered our minds that we were colored."[17] Artist and friend Mañuel Pardo explains that Ana was unprepared for the institutionalized racism that she found in the United States.[18] In one incident, for example, when their foster mother found money missing from her purse, she predictably suspected the two girls of theft. Ana's cousin Kaki recalls the letter the American priest sent to her family in Cuba, which stated that "the family that took them in, with benevolence and charity, has accused them of stealing." To their U.S. guardians they were, she concludes, "suspiciously Latin."[19] Pardo is convinced that it was because of the girls' dark coloring that "nobody wanted them." As a result, some of those who did wind up as their guardians behaved as though the girls were lucky to have anything at all.[20]

The girls' color, which was darker than that of most Iowans, who were of predominantly Northern European ancestry, made them increasingly the targets of racism. As the girls grew older, they became more acutely aware of their difference from their peers. It was in high school in the mid-1960s, Raquel reports, "that we first experienced racism from our peer group." She describes how Ana received anonymous phone calls in which she was called "nigger" and told, "Go back to Cuba, you whore!" Ana Mendieta later reported to Cuban television that, "since I look Latin, I was always 'la putica,' the little whore, to them."[21] Such frightening epithets were given an eerie weight by the civil rights struggle taking place.

In this period, with events such as the forced integration of the University of Mississippi and the passage of the Civil Rights Act of 1964, many whites became increasingly fearful of the loss of racial and social purity. Although she was not African in heritage, in this context Ana Mendieta's ethnicity and darker skin color made her racially spurious. In 1963, at an orphanage to which they had been transferred in Cedar Rapids, Iowa, the girls came in contact with a group of recently exiled Cuban boys who had just been sent to Iowa from Miami. The boys' vivid descriptions of violent class and race conflicts in the South so terrified the girls that, when told by Catholic Charities that they were to be sent to Miami to live with distant relatives, they wrote back begging not to go. Frightened by their potential proximity to a destructive political struggle in which they might be perceived as "niggers," they asked to remain where their experience of racism had at least not resulted in bodily injury. These and other experiences led Mendieta to want to dissociate herself from whiteness; she later identified herself as a "woman of color" and as "non-white."[22]

The circumstances of Mendieta's U.S. citizenship are important to understanding how she perceived her relation to this country. In 1966, five years after their arrival in the United States (Ana Mendieta was now seventeen years old), the girls' mother and younger brother, Ignacio, joined them, but the joy of their reunion was diminished by the fact that their father remained in Cuba, a prisoner of the Castro regime. After Ana's mother arrived in the United States, her one goal was to obtain her husband's release from prison. As Cuban citizens, she and her children had few rights and could not petition the U.S. government for help in the matter, so she was determined to become a legal citizen. After Ana and Raquel's experiences of abandonment, betrayal, disregard, incarceration, and racism in the United States, they were not especially anxious to declare their allegiance to it. Raquel in particular could not bear the idea, but she was convinced by Ana that they should apply for citizenship. Ana's rationale was that they would never be allowed to do anything freely or travel anywhere openly with only a Cuban passport. Ana told her sister, "I want to travel." It is ironic that, for Ana Mendieta, becoming a U.S. citizen was her only way of escaping what she felt was her incarceration in the United States. A few months after becoming a naturalized citizen in 1970, she took the first of several trips to Mexico. The girls did not see their father for nine more years (until April 1979), some eighteen years after they had said good-bye to him in Cuba.

It was against the backdrop of civil rights struggles, the women's liberation movement, and the increasing antagonism between the First World and the Third that Ana Mendieta formed her political views of her native country and the country in which she was a naturalized citizen. Angered by her experiences in the United States, and critical of its economic policies, which seemed to establish gross disparities between classes,[23] she considered herself a member of the Third World. In a catalog essay for an exhibition of Third World women artists, she wrote: "We of the Third World in the United States have the same concerns as the people of the Unaligned Nations. The white population of the United States, diverse, but of basic European stock, exterminated the indigenous civilization and put aside the Black as well as the other non-white cultures to create a homogenous male-dominated culture above the internal divergency [sic]."[24] Mendieta's statement seems to predict Trinh Minh-ha's often-quoted claim that there is "a Third World in the First World and vice versa."[25] It insists on the diversity and internal conflicts that are masked by notions like the people and nation. It exposes the patriarchal and colonial power that attends such homogenizing structures. How, then, did Mendieta use the earth to dramatize these issues, to make us hear the ambivalence in the voice that reads the nation's script?

When we look at the photograph that documents Mendieta's *First Silueta*, executed in a Zapotec tomb in Oaxaca, Mexico, in 1973, we witness her strategic representation of the earth (see pl. 8 on p. 38). Pointed downward, the camera captures Mendieta's vulnerable naked body lying covered in long stems and tiny white flowers at the bottom of a rocky tomb. She is surrounded by stones and dirt whose lifetimes constitute the geological calendar. Their dull ashen color strongly contrasts with the pale skin of her body, their roughness with the fragility of the green and white foliage.

The act of stripping off her clothes to climb down into the sepulchre engages a familiar set of binaries: essence/inessence, nature/culture, primitive/civilized, and cosmos/history. Of this piece, Mendieta writes, "I bought flowers at the market, lay in the tomb and was covered with white flowers. The analogy was that I was covered by time and history." [26] Her naked form is marked by age yet symbolizes an ageless femaleness; it is both bound to and free from time, particular and universal. She stands both for the real (herself at age twenty-five) and for the representational (an icon of primordial femaleness).

Mendieta's body is particular to the extent that it is marked by death. The photograph captures the light of that irretrievable moment, the fleeting aspect of the mortal body, the life that escapes with every breath. This body, soft with flesh, its limbs brightened by warm sunlight, is as transient as the delicate flowers that wilt even as the shutter clicks. As though in the tradition of seventeenth-century *vanitas* paintings, this *Silueta* reminds the viewer both of the threat of death and of the promise of rebirth. With each spring, the cycle of life is renewed.

Mendieta's body is universal to the extent that the ancient association between the female and the earth is inscribed on it. By climbing down and lying on the cold, rocky floor of this miniature stage and covering her body with freshly cut flowers, Mendieta trades on the viewer's understanding of the earth-as-woman metaphor: she brings forth and takes back life; she is natural and eternal; she is wild and in need of cultivation; she is both fruitful/sexual and barren/unyielding; she is the mother of us all.

For Mendieta, the earth is fundamentally defined as a primeval origin. It is constituted by a temporal relation with the body in which the earth is an eternal force prior to history and the mortal body is bound to time clocked by the earth's movements. Mendieta's earth thus falls under

Mircea Eliade's category the *primitive*; that is, it cannot be measured by history, only by cosmos, by the perpetual return to origin. Numerous statements in which she characterizes the earth as "primordial," "fundamental," "original," "prehistoric," and the body as contingent, tied to birth and death, reflect this aspect of Mendieta's philosophy. She writes, for example, "Through my art, I want to express the immediacy of life and the eternity of nature."[27] Such statements make evident that, for Mendieta, the body, the human, is bound to history, both to death and to culture. Because the earth supersedes history, it is extraordinarily powerful.

Lying in this tomb, Mendieta's body suggests the dichotomy of nature and culture, a dichotomy that is pictured in gendered terms. The tomb, an artifact of an ancient and highly developed civilization, is constructed of stones hewn from the earth, shaped, and arranged around a cubical cavity. Because it still existed in 1973 when Mendieta was photographed in it, some two thousand years after its construction, it has become a monument to Zapotec civilization. The tomb's cultural origins produce Mendieta's body as nature. By contrast with its squared edges and rough texture, her body appears soft and fragile; one empathetically feels the cold dirt floor, the pain of tender flesh lying on gravel. Representing nature as female, Mendieta's body has but a fragile, fleeting existence; the tomb as culture, by contrast, seems eternal and powerfully inevitable.

The nature/culture binary is constructed precisely on the model of cosmos/history or essence/antiessence that Eliade identifies. Anthropologist Sherry Ortner explains that culture, the masculine element of the pair, appears always to be more valued: "Thus culture . . . at some level of awareness asserts itself to be not only distinct from, but superior in power to, nature, and the sense of distinctiveness and superiority rests precisely on the ability to transform—to 'socialize' and 'culturalize'—nature."[28] The tomb is the most fundamental of culture's manifestations. It segregates the dead from the living, transcends disorder and decay, controls the body's grotesque putrefaction. Yet culture does not have the last word in Mendieta's performance, for, although its authority appears eternal relative to human mortality, that authority is measured by a clock set on galactic time. While the tomb itself is ancient, the stones of which it is composed predate it by aeons. Thus, the stones, the grave itself, and Mendieta's body lying in it tell a story of time and history, one that begins, not with Mendieta, or with Zapotec culture, but with the very formation of the earth. By performing this ritual of creation and destruction, death and regeneration, Mendieta claims the freedom of Eliade's "traditional man" to "annul his own history through periodic abolition of time." "This freedom," Eliade writes, "in respect to his own history—which, for the modern, is not only irreversible but constitutes human existence—cannot be claimed by the man who wills to be historical."[29] Nature is not weaker than culture; it is simply more patient.

Free, eternal, and powerful, the earth is the object of intense desire for Mendieta. She always casts it as something lost that must be regained: "My art is the way I re-establish the bonds that unite me to the Universe. It is a return to the maternal source. Through the making of earth/body works I become one with the earth. It is like being encompassed by nature, an after-image of the original shelter in the womb."[30] It is very common for critics to link statements such as this with the fact of Mendieta's expatriation. They read her desire to "re-establish" bonds as a result of having been forced into exile. Tuula Karjalainen, one of the organizers of Mendieta's recent exhibition in Finland, is the latest in a long line of writers to claim that, "separated from her country and cut off from her roots, Mendieta longed constantly for Cuba, as can be seen in her work. . . . Each piece of land she worked on became a substitute for her country."[31] Karjalainen reads the earth as a transcendent substitute for Mendieta's lost nation.

While this interpretation has some validity, it is truly useful only when it opens onto a more comprehensive analysis. If we consider this work a template for the earth as feminine, it is significant that Mendieta chose a Zapotec monument as its site. The Zapotecs, as Mary Sabbatino explains, "were the only Mesoamerican people who resisted the Aztecs. Their reclamation of identity and their rebellion against domination spoke to Mendieta of her own struggles."[32] The piece shows that the earth is never simply an enormous prehistoric womb; it is always also the subject of national, political, and patriarchal claims. It is, as a large number of Latino artists have shown, as much the object of colonial domination and plunder as gold and slaves. In this regard, Mendieta's work resonates with that of such artists as Josely Carvalho and Ismael Frigerio, who concern themselves with the commodification of Latin America's natural resources. It is clear that Mendieta's earth is neither general nor traditional; rather, it is deeply tied to colonial resistance. This earth is an enduring origin that manages to escape a foreign culture and an enslaving history.

Charles Merewether takes a step from Mendieta's personal experience of exile toward the hemispheric experience of colonization when he states pointedly that "Caribbean artists and writers, like Mendieta, have repeatedly addressed the trauma of deterritorialization reflected in the histories of their violent ejection from their homelands and by the culture of colonial slavery."[33] Merewether insists that Latin American political history must inform interpretations of this earth art. I want to beckon him toward an even broader understanding of the notion of *deterritorialization*. I would place more emphasis on Gilles Deleuze and Felix Guattari's use of that term, which, as Caren Kaplan explains, signifies "the displacement of identities, persons, and meanings that is endemic to the postmodern world system."[34] It seems to me that, by foregrounding the deracination of Latin American culture, Mendieta makes more than an anticolonialist plea, does more than protest the hybridization of the region's identity. She also deconstructs the purity of dominant Western identities that is secured by the constant representation of the subaltern as troubled victim.

This interpretation is borne out by the fact that Mendieta's statement paraphrases Octavio Paz, who writes that solitude is "a form of orphanhood, an obscure awareness that we have been torn from the All, and an ardent search: a flight and a return, an effort to re-establish the bonds that unite us with the universe."[35] All human beings are, for Paz, condemned to this solitude: identity is a perpetual searching for "country," for assimilation into the many. For Mendieta, the earth symbolizes the essence from and against which subjectivity is inevitably constructed—not just her own, not just Latin America's, but everyone's. By obsessively staging the ritual of return, Mendieta exposes the privilege of dominant culture to represent its own identity as untroubled.

Having claimed that, for Mendieta, the earth represents an essential origin, it is important to interrogate the terms by which that origin is commonly understood and to explore how she has reinscribed it. This may be achieved if we contextualize her work more fully and compare it to the efforts of another artist operating with similar themes and strategies. It will be useful, therefore, to compare a work by Mendieta to one by Mary Beth Edelson, a feminist artist who also works with issues surrounding the female body and the earth. Edelson took several photographs to document a performance she did in 1974 called *Woman Rising, Spirit*, in which she played the role of "Everywoman" (pl. 9). In this performance, executed in the Outer Banks of North Carolina, Edelson has photographed herself partially naked, standing in an iconic pose with arms upraised in a ritual gesture invoking the power of the "Great Goddess." She has literally transfigured herself by painting on her own body (embellishing her abdomen and nipples with concentric circles, drawing in a third eye) and by inscribing the photographic negative (making her hair into a medusan mane and encircling her head and chest in a mandorla, the radiating lines of which look like a child's drawing of the sun). "These photographic images," writes Edelson, "were defining images—not

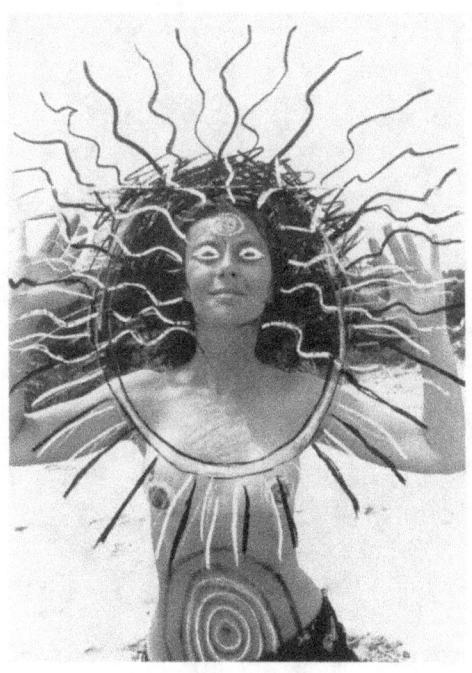

Plate 9. Mary Beth Edelson,
Woman Rising/Spirit, 1974.
Performance executed in the
Outer Banks, North Carolina.
Photograph and drawing by
Mary Beth Edelson. Courtesy
of the artist.

who I am but who *we are*. The images were presented aggressively as sexuality, mind and spirit in one body. I was summoning the Goddess to make house calls, talking to Goddess with the body, and ending the dialog with being. These rituals were photographic evidence of the manifestations and recognition of a powerful feminine force: Everywoman." [36] Edelson's photograph embodies her interests in goddess spiritualism and body art, strategies of 1970s feminism that focused on breaking out of patriarchy by locating a separate history of women, by reclaiming the female body, celebrating the maternal, and reevaluating long-held metaphoric connections between women and nature. The goddess is the personification of feminine power. The photograph is evidence of a specter, of a wavering and insubstantial presence, an untenable unity called *Everywoman*.

This image is very similar to a work that Mendieta produced in Iowa in 1977 as part of her *Tree of Life* series (pl. 10). As does Edelson, Mendieta stands naked in a frontal pose with upraised arms. This image, too, has been seen as representing a goddess, one in which the ties to nature are even more direct than in Edelson's work. Unlike Edelson, Mendieta has covered her body in mud and stands in miniature scale against an enormous tree. Instead of inscribing radiating lines of force on the image, lines that indicate the emanation of power, Mendieta draws her power

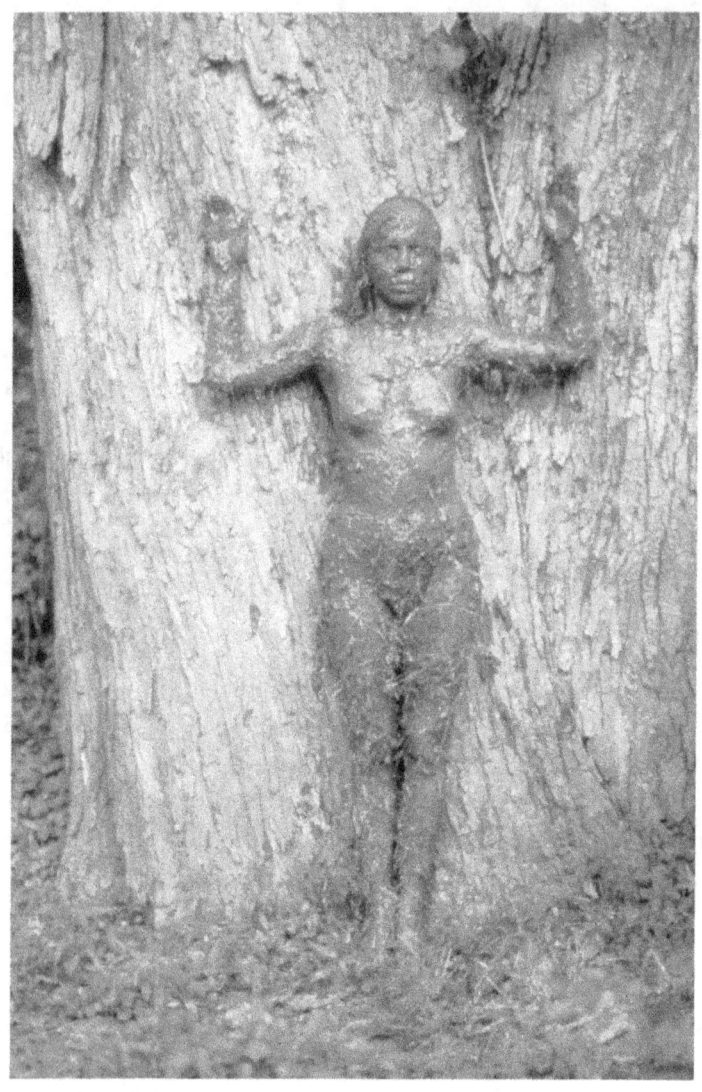

Plate 10. Ana Mendieta, untitled (*Tree of Life* series), 1977. Color photograph documenting performance in Iowa. Courtesy of the Estate of Ana Mendieta and Galerie Lelong, New York.

from the enormity of the tree behind her, from her near disappearance in nature. Mendieta's goddess does not exist independently of the earth; for her, the female body, the maternal, and origins were all tied directly to a land that is eternal, natural, and powerful.

Both works were generated in the light of a series of books appearing in the 1970s and 1980s that took up the subject of the earth and its relation to the feminine. Usually, such texts focused on the Great Goddess, an ancient mythological prototype from whom all women are said to descend. Mary Daly's *Beyond God the Father* (1973) and Merlin Stone's *When God Was a Woman* (1976), for example, were influential texts on this subject. Daly brought a feminist critique to Christianity, and Stone documented the history of paleolithic goddess imagery, suggesting that such images represented a prepatriarchal theology based on worship of the earth. This alternative history and philosophy was enormously important to early second wave feminists, who sought to recover a past that could empower their critique of patriarchy. Other books on the subject soon followed, such as Carol Christ and Judith Plaskow's *Womanspirit Rising: A Feminist Reader in Religion* (1979) and Christine Downing's *The Goddess: Mythological Images of the Feminine* (1981).[37]

The theory that fostered this flurry of publication is based on two potent notions of origin: the Great Goddess represents an "original" set of religious beliefs that has been suppressed by centuries of Judeo-Christian doctrine; the earth, which is incarnated in the goddess, is the ultimate and incontrovertible origin of life. As such, the female earth is given value as a transcendental signifier that supersedes the phallus. Mendieta integrated the power of origins into her works, which "recall prehistoric beliefs of an omnipresent female force whose body parts made the earth a living creature." "In essence," she explains, "my works are the reactivation of primeval beliefs at work within the human."[38]

A strong relation exists between the structure of *woman* as a category and that of *nation. Woman* refers both to an individual and to a group, to a collectivity that is achieved in spite of difference. As with *nation*, this concept is never secure; it never rests on either side of the equation but vacillates constantly back and forth. Edelson's character, Everywoman, embodies this narrative ambivalence; at one and the same time her character represents individual difference *and* monolithic unity. When Edelson appeals to "Everywoman," she represents Woman as a single unified essence but also women as a diverse group. This is where the character's power lies. Were it simply a shorthand for women as a divergent group (difference), it would not hold out the promise of empowerment that Edelson gives it. Likewise, if it simply represented a divine entity distinct from individual women (sameness), its "feminine force" would remain foreign and unattainable. Everywoman thereby binds together these terms, revealing their interdependence. Everywoman's story is "out of many, one."

Mendieta ciphers the equation differently. She too produces a unified picture of woman—a single female body baptized by earth in a time before history. This picture does not match Edelson's, however, and, as a result, it asks us to make room for two essences. Edelson is performing, in a theatrical sense, the character Everywoman, a fictional role for which she requires elaborate makeup. The lines radiating from her head and inscribed on her body, signifiers for an otherwise unrepresentable supernatural power, are decidedly artificial. Like theatrical costumes, props, or special effects, they draw attention to the powerful character they are meant to encode and away from the true identity of the performer. Mendieta, too, is costumed, her body clothed in mud, but her staging does not so much revive a familiar theatrical role as performatively rewrite one. Like the black actor who must redundantly wear blackface for a minstrel show in which he is forced to perform racist stereotypes, Mendieta colors her body with the earth to make color the subject of her act. Unlike him, however, she is not performing a grotesque simplification of identity meant to assuage the fears of a white audience. On the contrary, she is insisting that her audience see a color and an identity whose threatening potential it would otherwise like to forget.

Although relying herself on essentialist notions of woman and the primitive, Mendieta was strongly critical of those who envisioned Everywoman as white. She wrote in a catalog essay a few years after this performance: "During the mid to late sixties as women in the United States politicized themselves and came together in the Feminist Movement with the purpose to end the domination and exploitation by the white male culture, they failed to remember us. American Feminism as it stands is basically a white middle class movement. . . . This exhibition points not necessarily to the injustice and incapacity of a society that has not been willing to include us, but more towards a personal will to continue being 'other.' "[39] Here, she is again paraphrasing Octavio Paz, who writes of the pachuco: "The purpose of his grotesque dandyism and anarchic behavior is not so much to point out the injustice and incapacity of a society that has failed to assimilate him as it is to demonstrate his personal will to remain different."[40] What does it mean for her to compare herself to a pachuco, to a character who performs otherness, who is costumed in exile?

In part it means that, as a member of the Third World, her national and ethnic identity was illegible within the terms of U.S. feminism. As a result, she employed the pachuco's survival strategy "not of purity, of saying *less*, but rather of saying *more*, of saying too much, with the wrong accent and intonation, of mixing the metaphors, making illegal crossings, and continually transforming language so that its effects might never be wholly assimilable to an essential ethnicity."[41] She effectively inscribes herself within the position of exile, exile not only from her native country of Cuba but from the nation of woman, where, as a Latina, she is allowed little physical or ideological space. This forced her, sometime later, after having worked with A.I.R. for two years, to end her association with the cooperative feminist gallery.[42] She was furious with its predominantly white, middle-class membership and the unwillingness of some of its members to open up to a more diverse coalition.

Mendieta's performance of essence is meant to empower her exile from the nation of woman—her inability and lack of desire to call the white feminists' version of woman home. The narrative of this performance might be said to be rather a "counternarrative" of the nation, one that, in Bhabha's words, "continually evoke[s] and erase[s] its totalizing boundaries—both actual and conceptual—disturb[s] those ideological manoeuvres through which 'imagined communities' are given essentialist identities." Mendieta proves herself a supplement to the nation of woman. She exists on its margins, where she makes Bhabha's claim that, in the equation out of many, one, "adding 'to' need not 'add up' but may disturb the calculation."[43] In looking at Edelson's performance after having seen Mendieta's work, we are more likely to ask, "What does it mean for Mary Beth Edelson to perform Everywoman?" And we are more likely to answer that it makes whiteness universal, that it allows us to avoid the racial assumptions that are made in the name of woman.

While there is a tendency to separate the terms as mutually exclusive, it is important to recognize that *color, ethnicity, gender, nation,* and *earth* are all intertwined in Mendieta's work. In 1972, she did another performance in which she used a skeleton to evoke themes of death, rebirth, the earth, and the feminine (pl. 11). Performing naked, she arranged a human skeleton on the intensely green grass of a small clearing. Kneeling over the body, she sculpted a face by applying pale pink putty to the skull; then, in the same manner, she gave the figure hands. She then startlingly lay down on top of the skeleton, her brown skin covering its bleached white bones, her black hair obscuring the camera's view of the putty face, and gently placed her mouth over the pink lips of the body beneath her.

Lucy Lippard interprets this pivotal moment of the performance as

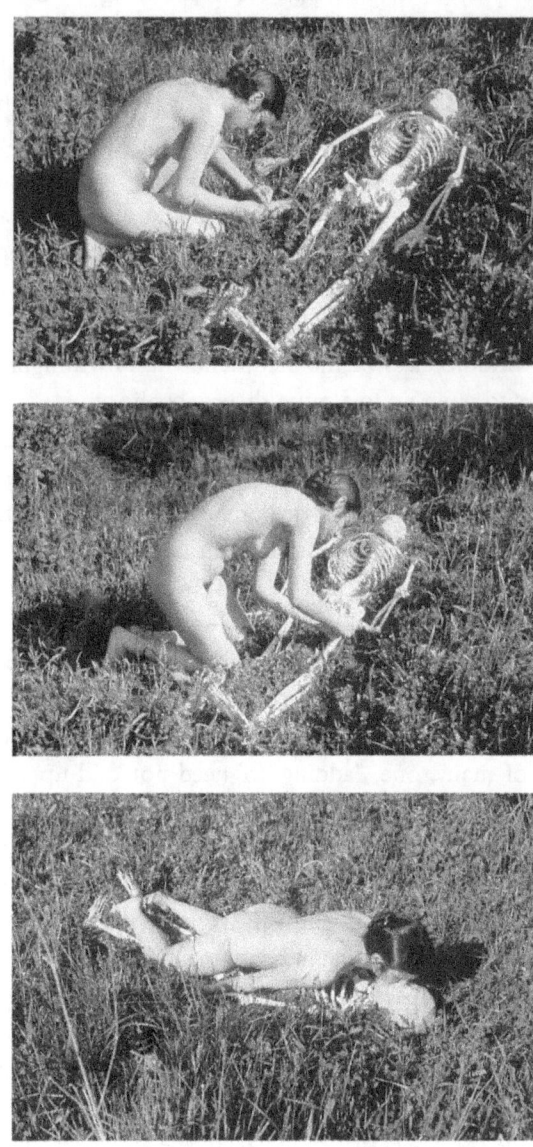

Plate 11. Ana Mendieta, untitled performance, 1972. Color
photographs documenting performance in Iowa City,
Iowa. Courtesy of the Estate of Ana Mendieta and Galerie
Lelong, New York.

Mendieta's having breathed life into the dead figure, suggesting that, in her resuscitating gesture, Mendieta's body covers over the skeleton as though it were buried.[44] This fleshy earth then breathes life into the body in a process of death and regeneration. To perform the earth as female is to rely on the same long-standing and complex metaphor that she used in her *First Silueta* (pl. 8 on p. 38), in which the female body as sign is inflected toward its most feral and fecund possibilities. This metaphor invests the female body with the very essence of nature: it is all womb and becoming, a rich humus for spontaneous and abundant growth and indiscriminate nurturing. It is also, at the same time, all tomb and decay, a crumbling and inevitable destination, the fulfillment of the process of bodily dissolution begun at the moment of separation from the mother. Earth and woman together represent both our origin and our fate. They share a sympathetic understanding of the cycles of life; indeed, they mark with their very "bodies" the passage of time.

In this work, however, the obvious romantic theme of the earth's regenerative power must yield to that of sexual desire. Mendieta's life-giving gesture is also a kiss, her covering of the body also a mounting that is both sexual and smothering. The work is vivid evidence of Mendieta's contention that her art is fundamentally about "Eros and life/death."[45] The earth's regenerative power must likewise yield to questions of racial identity since Mendieta's brown body is clearly meant to appear in contrast to the standard "flesh-colored" putty she has molded for the skeleton.

In this performance, Ana Mendieta unbaptizes the earth; that is, she relies on its seemingly fixed meanings while performatively producing their surplus. She unmarks the earth by presuming its association with the female, its opposition to culture, its primitiveness, and its role in both life and death. By essentializing the earth, she attempts to save it from culture, remove it from language, ideology, and politics. Once "safe" in this depoliticized site, Mendieta tries to re-mark its essence in unexpected terms. What happens to our centuries-old view of "Mother Earth" if we are forced to consider the possibility of a sexualized mother, of an entity whose procreativity is the result, not of maternalism, but of sexual desire? What happens when we are forced to interrogate our presumption that the word *earth* (like the word *mankind*) is universal? What if the unmarked whiteness of the earth were marked with color?

Mendieta's performance does not merely reenact a familiar story; it is neither simply mimetic nor simply descriptive in Austin's sense.[46] Although we might be tempted to think that she is acting the role of the "earth," she is actually acting *on* the earth, making it into something new.

Her actions are performative to the extent that they reconstitute the very terms around which they are organized. In this way, Mendieta repeats the earth/woman metaphor while relying on the discursive power it inherits from the past. At the same time, she turns against this inheritance. Her retelling of the metaphor is a repetition with a difference.

The seemingly obsessive repetition of the female form that is enacted in her *Silueta* series prompts Mira Schor to critique Mendieta's work as an uncomplicated, generic treatment of femininity.[47] Repetition, it is important to note, is an extremely important component of the performative. It is only through repetition that one draws on the authority of established metaphor, well-worn rhetoric, accepted discourse. In another work from the *Silueta* series, executed in Iowa in 1977, Mendieta used her plywood silhouette to make a shallow impression in snow (pl. 12). At first, the figure appears as though it were embossed on white paper. The pale blue shadows on the snow created by the figural depression are subtle. As time passed, the indentation melted more rapidly than the snow by which it was surrounded. Eventually, the *Silueta* revealed a patch of dark grass and leaves in the shape of Mendieta's body, which was outlined in white.

The same set of binaries operates here as did in her other works: birth/death, nature/culture, female/male, and time/timelessness. As with the earlier works, which engaged the process of birth and decay, this work repeats the cyclic process by which the seasons are arranged and by which water circulates through condensation, freezing, precipitation, thawing, and evaporation. By marking the snow and watching it melt, Mendieta places the body in the death of winter and the rebirth of spring.

Mendieta also troubles the very metaphors she cites. The work is not just about the seasons or the land but about the ways in which both are invested with racial, ethnic, and hemispheric associations. Despite its momentary possession by the white snow, the earth has an undying bond with the "colored" peoples who once inhabited it. This work (as well as the others that Mendieta constructed in snow and ice) is rarely referred to and has only recently been published. Perhaps this is because such pieces do not seem to fit the idea of Mendieta as a "Cuban" or a "Latina" and the stereotypes of tropical hot-bloodedness with which those identities are associated.

Read in these terms, the work displays her awareness of such stereotypes as revealed in yet another transformation; the body that it represents changes from white to brown, from cold to warm. As with the skeleton piece, this work asks us to consider the earth in racial terms, where race is understood to be elusive and changing. That is a hard concept for those of

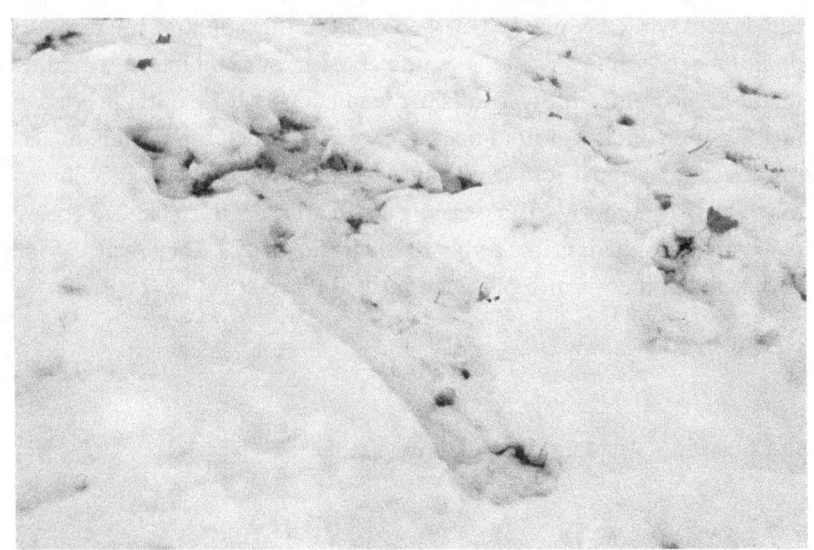

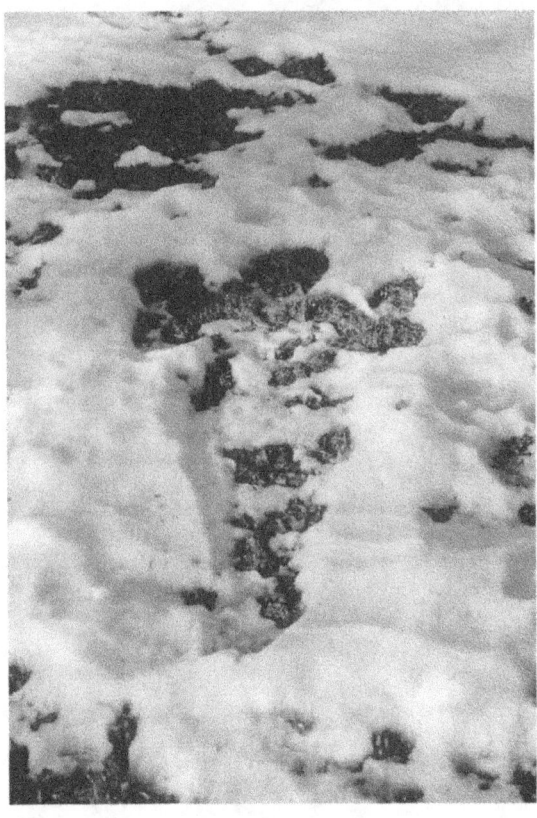

Plate 12. Ana
Mendieta, untitled
(*Silueta* series), 1977.
Color photographs
documenting
earth/body work
executed in Iowa.
Courtesy of the Estate
of Ana Mendieta and
Galerie Lelong,
New York.

us who are white because, when we say *race* in this country, we generally do not mean "white." White goes unmarked in our culture, its meanings unquestioned, its stability assumed. Mendieta uses the natural process of melting and condensation to mark the ways in which the earth is subject to racial and national authority, but she also uses it to reveal the vulnerability of that authority. *Race, ethnicity,* and *gender* are unstable categories; trying to grasp them is like trying to catch snowflakes. They melt as soon as they touch the warmth of the body, the heat retained by the earth.

Chapter 3

EXILE

We must leave home, as it were, since our homes are often sites of racism, sexism, and other damaging social practices. —Caran Kaplan, "Deterritorializations"

My great-grandfather came to Iowa from Germany in 1866. He married, built a large white clapboard house with a garden and an orchard, and planted six pine trees in front of the house for each of his six children. The trees, which have now surpassed the house in their enormity, represent the claim of my family on that place. They mark a spot of origination from which all the subsequent generations have been born. Even more than the house itself, the trees declare ownership of that land; their roots push down deep into the earth, forcefully making it home. It is a place that is, to use Sigmund Freud's term, *heimlich*, a word whose proper usage he exemplifies in the sentences, "I have roots that are most *heimlich*. I am grown in the deep earth." [1] For me Iowa is "homely"; it is a place I thought I knew.

What has shaken my familiarity with this place is a trifle, a small mound of sand that Ana Mendieta once formed into the shape of a body

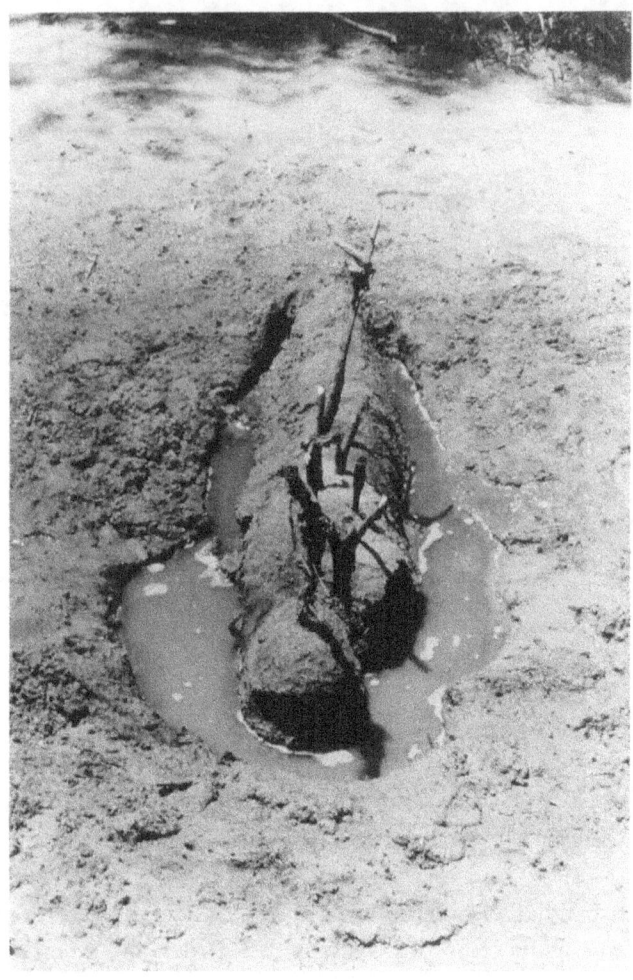

Plate 13. Ana Mendieta, untitled (*Fetish* series), 1977. Color photograph
of earth/body work with mud, water, and sticks, executed at Old
Man's Creek, Iowa, 20 × 13¼ inches, no. 2/2. Collection of the
Whitney Museum of American Art, New York. Courtesy of the Estate
of Ana Mendieta and Galerie Lelong, New York.

on the bank of an Iowa creek (pl. 13). She dug a shallow moat around the body so that, in the photograph of the piece, it appears to rest in a small pool of water. She pierced the figure, whose arms, legs, and face remain unarticulated, with sticks of various lengths. Like arrows, their aim is true; they project vertically from the body where they have struck the head and torso. This work, from Mendieta's *Fetish* series (1976), might as well be a sand castle for all the difference it has made to the surrounding landscape, yet I am compelled to imagine what it must have been like to walk in the area and stumble on this body molded of wet brown sand. It unnerves me. It is an entirely alien configuration that disrupts the horizon and defamiliarizes the land.

It does not make me feel at home; rather, it functions something like Freud's *unheimlich* or uncanny, which he describes as "nothing new or alien, but something that is familiar and old-established in the mind and that has become alienated from it only through the process of repression."[2]

Despite the risks presented by invoking Freud, his explanation of the heimlich/unheimlich is enormously useful. With it, he teaches us that home is a concept related both to feelings of belonging and to repressed memories of alienation. His is also an efficient model for thinking about the politics of location in psychic as well as geographic terms. Significant to Freud's discussion of the heimlich and the unheimlich are their sets of distinct yet overlapping characteristics. The heimlich has two valences, one of which signifies home but also belonging, familiarity, intimacy, and a sense of comfort. Heimlich's other valence is something like privacy or that which is concealed or kept from sight.[3]

The unheimlich is a sensation produced by time and remembrance. First, it describes the flood of repressed memories that fill the subject with dread as he encounters some seemingly unrelated object or person.[4] Freud proposes another category of sensation to which the unheimlich refers—the double—that manifests itself in both objects and events. The double can refer to the coincidental recurrence of the same set of events or to those nonliving characters such as ghosts, dolls, or souls that are nonetheless animate and seem to duplicate human life.[5] I want to emphasize that it is precisely the sense of familiarity (homeliness) perceived in regard to the double (the uncanny) that for Freud causes our discomfort. These two conflicting sensations are inherent in Freud's definition of the heimlich: it is both familiar and secret. Thus, the heimlich always bears within itself the quality of the unheimlich.

The figure on the creek's bank produces a feeling of the uncanny primarily because it is a "double," a totemic body built to human scale. More specifically, it is a "fetish," endowed with magical powers. In describing this work in an interview, Mendieta explains: "I made an image out of sand and stuck pieces of wood in it . . . it was a fetish piece. That summer my mother had a cancer operation and I didn't consciously set out to help her, I just did the piece, but I think it was connected to death imagery." Whether consciously produced to help her mother or not, the piece is meant to duplicate a living body; it is, therefore, a ghostly double, an object that is unheimlich. As a double of Mendieta's mother, it is prone, wounded, and fragile. Its imminent dissolution and inevitable return to the sand that surrounds it parallel human mortality. As Mendieta suggests, "I don't think you can separate death and life."[6] This piece, which calls forth life and prefigures death, ambivalently produces both the heimlich and its opposite; it prompts a sense of familiarity with death.

The work may also be considered unheimlich in that it forces an encounter with childhood memories long since repressed. Mendieta's earthen figure is familiar to me; I know that brown sand, the long green grasses on the banks of Iowa creeks, the dried sticks fallen from nearby trees. But something about this body is alien to me; it is marked by its configuration as foreign. At first, it might seem that the figure itself is alien in that one does not generally see bodies molded of sand and impaled with sharp sticks scattered about the Iowa landscape.

Yet to see this work solely as foreign, in that it seems to refer to some unknown "primitive" or ritualistic practice, is limiting. Rather, like Freud's unheimlich or uncanny, this work is alien, foreign, and unfamiliar because its presence alters a place of intense familiarity. It is not so much the figure itself but the landscape surrounding it that I no longer recognize. My experiences of Iowa do not bond me to Ana Mendieta; on the contrary, in her art they become meaningless. This work makes me alien. It makes me feel, however briefly, that I no longer belong here, that I can no longer lay claim to this place. The old house is reduced to ashes, the trees uprooted.

In Freud's terms, the feelings inspired by Mendieta's sand sculpture are the effect of repressed anxieties that, when faced with an uncanny strangeness, are brought to light. The anxiety that I am made to feel is a product of memory. I remember Iowa's landscape, growing up there, wading in creeks, smelling the fishy water, and playing with sand, sticks, leaves, and berries. Deeper than these physical sensations, I remember a sense of belonging, a sense of home. Deeper still, my memories unearth what had remained secret—that time when my idea of self was produced in relation to this home. Mendieta thus reveals my identity as a regulatory structure; she denaturalizes, makes strange the self that I have constructed on the site called *home*.

Freud explains these sensations in psychological terms when he claims that they can be produced by "a harking-back to particular phases in the evolution of the self-regarding feeling, a regression to a time when the ego had not yet marked itself off sharply from the external world and from other people."[7] The feeling of "uncanny strangeness" is caused, then, by my remembering myself as a stranger, by my remembering that my "self-regarding feeling" is only a tenuous fiction created long ago out of narratives such as family, home, landscape, and country.

The repressed thought that this work forces to the surface is that I have no claim on this land, that I am, not unlike Mendieta herself, an exile here, and that only the amnesia-producing mythologies of *America* and *whiteness* allow me to ignore this fact. The work plays in the dirt of my country, which, as we saw in the last chapter, is not as innocent an endeavor as one might at first imagine because, by playing in the dirt, it also plays in ideology. It makes me question what is meant by the discourses of "home," "exile," "nation," and "land" and, along with these, concepts of belonging, borders, margins, and centers. In unmooring these notions and denaturalizing their meanings, Mendieta's work usurps the hegemony that such ideas exercise; that is, her work makes me a spectator to my own exile.[8] I am no longer concerned to answer the question, "Where is Ana Mendieta?" Rather, I am forced to ask, "Where am I?"

This chapter will add to the argument already put forth that, by its references to the earth, Ana Mendieta's work is necessarily involved in the production of ideologies of the nation and that the earth as a category is always and everywhere inflected by this, its binary opposite. Moreover, in the previous chapter, I suggested that Mendieta played between earth and nation, essence and inessence, the one and the many. In this chapter, I name that "between," that limen, *exile*. By engaging the contradictions of identificatory practice relative to the female, the primitive, earth, and nation, Mendieta occupies the discursive position of exile, and she uses this position to produce in us a sense of the uncanny. She uses, in other words, exile performatively to question the limits and fixity of identity.

My argument will, therefore, be slightly different from the ones commonly made on Mendieta's behalf. As I explained earlier, critics have often (and with damaging results) seen her art as a direct manifestation of her own traumatic experiences of expatriation. Other critics have made more sophisticated analyses in which Mendieta becomes emblematic of what

Charles Merewether calls "the dialectics of exile." He argues that Mendieta's work "occupies a borderland, homelessness, wandering, a solitude that yearns for an imagined community, yet yields to living out a community of absence."[9] Unfortunately, the power of this kind of claim is often limited by confining its application to the experience of refugees alone. While critics may draw attention to the important historical and political context of this work, if they see in it only the trauma, dislocation, and subjugation of Latinity, they may ultimately reinforce the stereotype that white Western identities are clear, unproblematic, and fixed.

I want to think a little more carefully about the meanings of the nation and exile, to consider the ways in which Mendieta's exile is rhetorically constructed, through both narrative and performance, and to show how she works with and against this construction. I will claim that she understood exile as Octavio Paz did, not just as the loss of country, but as the lifelong process of coming to terms with the estrangement that is the soul of identity. To exemplify this process, I will focus on a story about African tribeswomen who eat dirt, which, I will argue, Mendieta retells in order to inscribe the story with the politics of identity.

Since this chapter is concerned with the category *home* and the strange feelings of alienation that discredit its coherence, it is necessary to understand what *home* means and how it is constructed. I am using *home* as a holophrastic term for the discourses of nation, the land, and identity, rather than as a metaphor for the domestic sphere. The representation of nation as home imbues nationhood with strong emotional associations. It becomes a powerful narrative that, as Timothy Brennan reminds us, "is a trope for such things as 'belonging,' 'bordering,' and 'commitment'" and that takes on "religion's concern with death, continuity, and the desire for origins."[10]

How the nation comes to have these associations can perhaps be explained by establishing its working definition. Benedict Anderson's seminal text *Imagined Communities* takes as its point of departure the very question of how the nation has come to have such emotional, political, and religious meanings. He wonders what it is about the nation that leads people willingly to give up their lives for it. Anderson conceptualizes the nation as an "imagined community" in the sense that it is invented or created rather than falsely fabricated. He writes, "It is *imagined* because the members of even the smallest nation will never know most of their fellow-members, meet them, or even hear of them, yet in the minds of each lives the image of their communion."[11]

Anderson's definition is significant and useful here, first, because it suggests that the nation is a symbolic rather than a geographic space and, second, because it proposes that *nation* is produced performatively. The nation is imagined by the individual but produced in communion with others; it is both conceived in the mind and performed in the body. It is performative because it gains force as a form of what Judith Butler has called *authoritative speech*: "I pledge allegiance to the flag. . . ." To these notions I would add another, one that has particular significance for a discussion of nation in Mendieta's work. The performance of nation is staged in the "land"—an ideological location bound up with both actual soil and emotional feelings prompted by the familiarity of landscape.

The power of all these elements—community, the body, land, and the familiar—safeguards the representation of home from close scrutiny and preserves its categorical purity and rhetorical force. As the antithesis of home, Freud's unheimlich/uncanny seems uniquely suited to question its discursive production of identity and origins. Indeed, if one accepts the idea of nation as home, the "unhomely" might seem to serve as its other, as the most powerful source of its deconstruction, but this is not entirely the case.

Here, it is necessary to reiterate an important feature of Freud's heimlich/unheimlich binary, one that makes it useful to the discussion of nation. Freud's attraction to these words and his extensive etymological research are the result of their curious duplicity. *Heimlich*, according to Freud, "finally coincides with its opposite, *unheimlich*."[12] It is, after all, familiarity, "homeliness," that produces the uncanny; the unheimlich lives at home. It would be misguided, then, to conceive of these words as antonyms, as dichotomous. It is not even as though they are tied together in the manner of other binaries, for, although at times they seem to signify opposites, they are actually one and the same.

Thus, the notion of heimlich/unheimlich is a template for understanding the equivocal construction of nation/exile. Placing these terms in opposition is the more commonly understood conception of nationhood, but it is one that hegemonically preserves the nation's conceived purity by defining it against a category perceived to be more complex and unstable. Using Freud's template, however, allows me to challenge this familiar model and claim instead that exile can be felt most keenly within one's national borders, indeed, that the very possibility of imagining the nation depends on the exilic. In this sense, the subversive power of exile can be realized only when it is recognized as one of the nation's constituent parts.

Both Julia Kristeva and Homi Bhabha have recently suggested that the uncanny is an intrinsic element of the ambivalent narrative of the nation.

Bhabha proposes that the uncanny is a metaphor for the contradictory narrative that conceives of society as a clearly defined totality while simultaneously revealing inherent anxieties over societal boundaries.[13] In this sense, the uncanny may be thought of as a manifestation of the anxieties that are both repressed and made evident in nationalism. Kristeva's argument involves a more strictly psychoanalytic reading in which the uncanny plays itself out between self and other. Hers is a more intimate version of Bhabha's notion of narrative ambivalence. For Kristeva, the feeling of uncanny strangeness is produced by the encounter with a foreigner and the subsequent awareness of one's own foreignness. Kristeva writes: "Confronting the foreigner whom I reject and with whom at the same time I identify, I lose my boundaries, I no longer have a container, the memory of experiences when I had been abandoned overwhelm me, I lose my composure. I feel 'lost,' 'indistinct,' 'hazy.' "[14] Kristeva accurately describes my feelings of anxiety over Mendieta's fetish piece; returned by memory to that time when identity was formed, I am overwhelmed. It is significant that Kristeva's description of confronting a foreigner is cast in terms of location; one's "boundaries" disappear, and one feels "lost." It is in the encounter with others that one's identity is formed; it is this performative engagement that produces or disrupts borders.

While slightly different in their emphasis, both Kristeva and Bhabha conceive of nation as a site of repression, which the question of identity troubles. Their descriptions of the uncanny are important in relation to my claims for Mendieta's earthworks because they form a discursive bridge between Freud's notion of the heimlich and Anderson's theories of the nation. They contribute significantly to Anderson's definition of nation by discussing it more specifically in terms of its repressed sense of alienation, its relation to identity, and its psychic manifestations. By doing this, Bhabha and Kristeva reveal a crack in the nation's authority and suggest a means by which the subaltern may be conceived as something more than simply victim of its machinations. In their interpretations, the exile/foreigner/alien poses a threat to the nation's coherence.

In order to consider the meanings produced by Mendieta's works, we cannot avoid the subject of exile. That Mendieta was sent to the United States from Cuba in 1961 at the age of twelve is the founding narrative of her biography; she constantly referred to it, and others followed suit, generating texts that explain her art, her life, and, even in some cases, her death in terms of exile. Here are but a few examples of this ubiquitous phenomenon:

Her sense of loss and deracination were the sources of her ongoing *silueta* series.

[Mendieta] uses her work as a means of establishing a 'sense of being,' of healing the 'wound' of separation.

Perceiving herself as in exile, Mendieta used her art to heal herself, thus provoking and perhaps healing others.[15]

In these narratives, her life rarely begins with her birth in Cuba; rather, it begins with the moment of her travel from there to here. Artist and critic Coco Fusco, herself a Cuban American, has gone so far as to say that "Ana *began her life* as a foreigner in relative isolation."[16] It is as though she sprang to life during this passage, as though she were born under the sign of movement; her progress through space has marked her irrevocably as a being in flux. She wrote often, as did critics, of her ambiguous position; she said in an interview, "I am between two cultures—you know?"[17]

The untenable position *between* is almost always judged to be a failure, an inability to complete the full circuit and return "home." A vocabulary of displacement, absence, and loss appears in discussions of both her life and her work. John Perreault is one of a number of critics who have attempted to explain her earth sculptures in these terms. He has written that they "helped her heal herself, if only temporarily. If one could claim even a small portion of the earth as one's own territory, exile was assuaged."[18] She was, according to most writers, digging in the dirt to find something she had lost, digging to plant her own roots so as to resist the forces of movement. She was trying to shake off that uncanny feeling and make her exile more "homely." Mendieta has herself confirmed this notion. "I work with the earth," she writes; "I make sculptures in the landscape. Because I have no motherland, I feel a need to join with the earth, to return to her womb."[19] She seems to borrow Freud's own definition of the heimlich: "I have roots that are most *heimlich*. I am grown in the deep earth."

Why did Mendieta constantly ascribe the meaning of her works to her exile? Why did she insist on being a foreigner? What was the effect of her works in a land to which she did not belong, a country in which she claimed citizenship only to escape its borders? By persistently referring to herself as homeless, Mendieta performs in the limen, not only between nations, but between ethnicities, races, and identities. By repeating the story over and over in interviews, catalog entries, and personal notes, Mendieta performatively produces herself as an exile. By repeating her stories in their own narratives, Mendieta's critics and historians enter into this performative; their descriptions gain, to use Butler's phrase, "the historicity of force."

By claiming that her works can help her overcome exile, she seems to suggest that they can produce the heimlich, a sense of familiarity, belonging, and home. Because of the overlapping nature of the heimlich and the unheimlich, this cannot be all there is to these figures, the many bodies that Mendieta carved and molded in earth that dotted the landscape of the United States.[20] That is, by putting down her roots in the earth, Mendieta also changes the landscape and makes it unfamiliar. If John Perreault is right in saying that her work is meant to cure her of the illness of exile, this cure is possible only by means of questioning the authority of the nation and making the viewer foreign in a familiar place.

Mendieta's exploration of and search for the earth does not represent the claiming of a small bit of territory, an attempt to fix herself in one country. On the contrary, with respect to nationality, the earth can provide only the possibility of flux. The earth is not a place but a ubiquitous concept, one that makes national identification uncanny. That is, to identify herself with the "earth" and not with either Cuba or the United States means that Mendieta can sustain rather than assuage exile. She can make exile home. By searching for her roots in the earth and not in country, she can claim an identity anywhere. Her imagined community crosses all territories, escapes all border guards, can be found anywhere on the planet, is tied neither to language nor to race. As Gloria Anzaldúa writes, "The skin of the earth is seamless. The sea cannot be fenced, el mar does not stop at borders."[21]

Mendieta's 1976 Silueta, executed on Mexico's shore, is a vivid demonstration of this notion (pl. 14). Here Mendieta traces her familiar silhouette and fills it with clusters of small red flowers.[22] As the tide rises, it slowly bisects the flowery body, leaving it marked by a visible border. Inasmuch as this is an "earthwork," its meanings depend on two different notions of earth, notions that roughly parallel the structure of the heimlich/unheimlich. On the one hand, earth can mean "land," "soil," or "landscape" and, more specifically, "homeland," "national soil," etc. In this sense, the figure that Mendieta carved into the beach in Mexico is a means of claiming a territory, of assuaging exile by making the landscape heimlich. This interpretation is most familiar to critics: Mendieta, exiled from Cuba, becomes a citizen of the United States solely in order to escape it. She goes to another Latin country in order to find a home, a familiar landscape, a sense of belonging.[23] There, the figure she inscribes

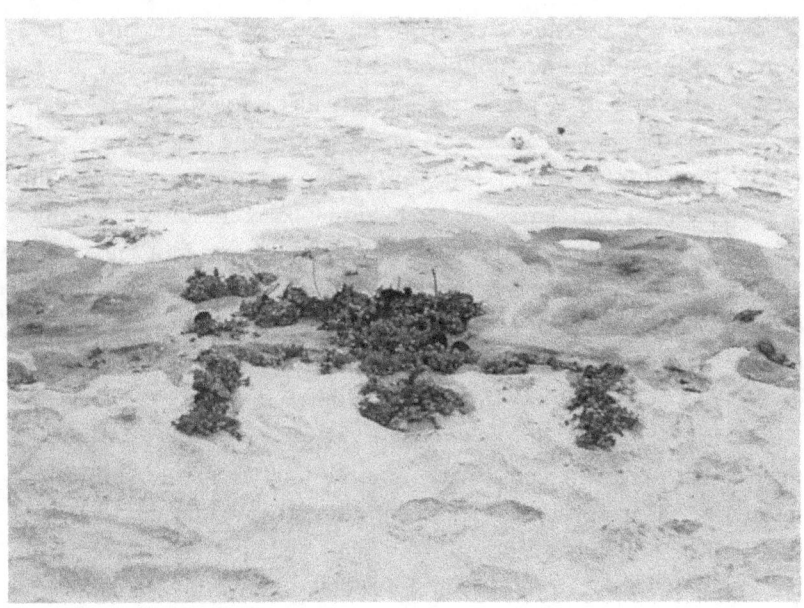

Plate 14. Ana Mendieta, untitled (*Silueta* series), 1976. Color photograph documenting earth/body work with sand, water, and flowers, executed in Salina Cruz, Mexico, 13 ¼ × 20 inches, edition of twenty. Courtesy of the Estate of Ana Mendieta and Galerie Lelong, New York.

is marked by a national border; it is positioned at the very place where Mexico as a nation begins and ends.

On the other hand, *earth* can also mean the planet earth, the globe. In this sense, Mendieta's figure is marked, not by a national boundary, but by a geological one. The tide forcefully reclaims it from the defining power of a national border, whose shifting nature the water makes evident. In this sense, the figure is a means of representing the futility of territory; it is a reminder of the unheimlich. The photograph documenting this process leaves the viewer with a dramatic picture of a body brutally divided in half by the earth's forces. This "earth" is both dirt and spherical planet, and it is still more. It is a living organism—powerful, shifting, capable of summoning water and wind. It is a sentient being whose desire makes paltry our own.

Although we tend most often to think of the earth, or earth as planet, in terms of its constantly shifting geography and the entrenchment of political factions, it actually supersedes such transient claims. In this sense, it has become a modern trope for the insolubility of contemporary problems; we now live in a global economy, have global communications, and foresee the possibility of global destruction. We have already seen that rhetorically to posit the earth as planet is to establish the "natural" in opposition to the artificiality of the nation. The effectiveness of the environmentalist movement, for example, depends on the ability to think beyond national boundaries and imagine a global community committed to nature. In appealing to the "earth," Mendieta refers, not only to dirt or land, but to the planet earth, to its natural, essential, and transcendent qualities. To embrace this earth is to embrace a life of exile, for the earth is uncanny; its meanings are both dependent on and independent of the nation. As a citizen of the earth, one is both at home and homeless.

Instead of attempting to overcome it, Mendieta appears to have held tight to her exile. She consistently referred to it as a source of artistic inspiration, as when she wrote: "Having been torn from my homeland (Cuba) during my adolescence I am overwhelmed by the feeling of having been cast out of the womb (Nature). My art is the way I re-establish the bonds that unite me to the Universe."[24] To insist on one's own foreignness as Mendieta did is to insist on exile as a true utopia. It is a no place that Mendieta nonetheless forcefully occupied. Kristeva explains such tenacity when she writes of the exile: "No obstacle stops him, and all suffering, all insults, all rejections are indifferent to him as he seeks that invisible territory, that country that does not exist but that he bears in his dreams, and that must indeed be called a beyond."[25] Mendieta's works always point to this "beyond," this place that is always deferred yet disturbingly always in the process of being located. As John Perreault writes, "Perhaps she had become addicted to exile."[26]

A 1980 work titled *Isla*, from Mendieta's *Silueta* series, illustrates this point (pl. 15). In this piece, she carved a female figure out of the mud of a shallow Iowa creek. *Isla* serves as one of the clearest examples of Mendieta's awareness of, and engagement with, issues of the nation. The island is a potent symbol of nation because its inherent and easily visible boundedness suggests both a natural geographic formation and a political territory. The island is exemplary of the unified and sovereign space that, through the collective imagination, becomes a nation. Furthermore, this island has obvious significance in relation to Mendieta's own Cuba. It is difficult, indeed, to look at this *isla* and not think at once of *la isla de Cuba*, to see in it a nation and an identity. It is a map of Cuba made in the mud of Iowa and as a result is neither here nor there; it is a body in exile. More specifically, it is a female body, which in Freud's theory is a primary source of the uncanny.[27] The female is a familiar foreigner, an ir-

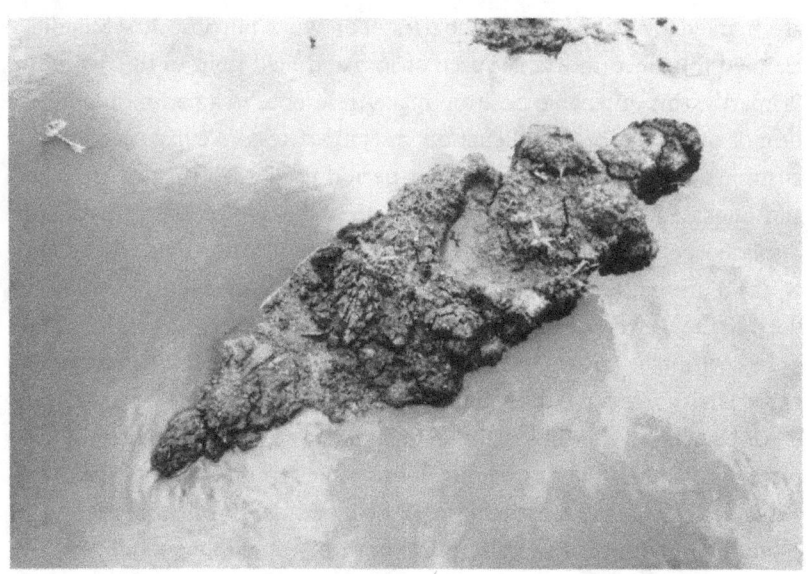

Plate 15. Ana Mendieta, *Isla* (*Silueta* series), 1981. Black-and-white photograph documenting earth/body work with earth and water executed outside Iowa City, Iowa, dimensions unknown. Courtesy of the Estate of Ana Mendieta and Galerie Lelong, New York.

reconcilable other. In this sense, to make an island of the female body is to symbolize femininity's exile. It is also to suggest the unique power of women, specifically, in their role as mothers, to produce the unheimlich. This gets us back to Octavio Paz and the question of solitude: the struggle for identity begins at the moment one is separated from the mother.

Mendieta's insistence on exile in her writings and artworks reflects not merely a longing for home but a simultaneous questioning of assimilation and foreignness. Edward Said helps explain the uses of exile when he writes, "Clutching difference like a weapon to be used with stiffened will, the exile jealously insists on his right to refuse to belong."[28] Mendieta's work evinces a similar stubbornness insofar as it insists on its own foreignness while simultaneously succumbing to environmental forces that will reintegrate it with the surrounding landscape. In these terms, her works seem literally caught in between. In addition to their thematic investment in exile, nation, and earth, Mendieta's earthworks also maintain a methodological investment in these issues. Her works are identities asserted in opposition to the land at the same time as their very structure is dedicated to dissolution and reassimilation with it.

What is meant by this body of decaying works that both mark and are marked by territorial boundaries? For what purpose has Mendieta claimed this uncomfortable space of loss and held tight to this weapon? Primarily, this untenable position makes reference to a common perception of our era as one of alienation; as Said writes, "We have become accustomed to thinking of the modern period itself as spiritually orphaned and alienated." Said adds, "Ours is indeed the age of the refugee, the displaced person, mass immigration."[29] Viewed in this light, Mendieta's works represent her sense of cultural and national alienation, thereby reflecting the universal phenomenon that Said describes.

In addition to this analysis, I want to suggest, not only that these works show what exile looks like, but that they are also capable of producing it for their viewers. This claim returns to my own experience of displacement at the sight of Mendieta's *Fetish;* she reminds me of the exile in which I share, of the sense that the growing emphasis on globalization in economics, politics, and culture has both disrupted and reinforced the discourse of national identity. The works' most profound effect is to be located, not in their seeming sympathy with their viewers' experience, or in their reassurance that we are not alone in our alienation, but in their ability to produce this very sense of loss and orphanhood in us. In this, they satisfy the terms of the performative. They do not merely perform, that is, describe or mimic, Mendieta's experience of exile. Rather, they "put into effect the relation they name"; they produce the condition, however fleeting, of the exilic.

Said explains this rather complicated claim when he writes, "Perhaps this is the only way to comprehend the most poignant of exile's fates, which is to be exiled by exiles, and to be condemned, seemingly without respite to continue to be exiled by exiles."[30] The persistent characterization of Mendieta's work as signifying her personal loss, a loss forced on a member of the so-called Third World by the West, works only to rehearse the script of dominance and submission on which both colonialism and imperialism are based. This narrative is a microcosm of those that always cast the person from the "underdeveloped country" as a naive victim. What Said is suggesting, on the contrary, is that, in the postcolonial world, the effect of colonialism is anything but restricted to the "Third World." It is, instead, revisited on those in power in complex relation within which the "First World" becomes victimized by its own imperialist policies. Said points to the continued struggles between Israel and Palestine as just one example of this; Israel, a nation of exiles, forces Palestine into exile.

In this regard, although Mendieta was forced by others into exile, and although she did experience intense feelings of loss and mutilation as a result, she cannot be considered only another victim of U.S. imperialism. The U.S. policy regarding Cuba has indeed meant devastation to the island, untold human suffering, the breakup of families, and the usurpation of ethnic identity, but it has at the same time produced a substantial population of Cuban immigrants who have changed, in a variety of ways far too complex to enter into here, the character of the United States. Like the return of the repressed, every new wave of immigrants to this country forces the question of the national identity, not of their native country, but of the nation whose identity we pretend to know. Mendieta's works are a visual reminder of these cultural negotiations.

Now that I have broadly laid out the terms of this discussion, I would like to focus on a specific narrative of nationhood that will pinpoint these themes. Mendieta's performance of exile may be fruitfully considered through a story she tells about women who eat dirt.[31] She pirates this story from the discourse of anthropology and mobilizes its rhetoric of "primitivism" toward her own ends. However, it is not enough to say that, in her concern with and writings about "primitive" cultures, Mendieta *uses* ethnography; rather, I would suggest that she *does* ethnography, in a specifically performative sense.

By repeating anthropological narratives, Mendieta engages their performativity and participates in the negotiation of their meanings. James Clifford's definition of *ethnography*, which he sees as "a performance emplotted by powerful stories," reinforces this interpretation. "Embodied in written reports," he adds, "these stories simultaneously describe real cultural events and make additional, moral, ideological, and even cosmological statements."[32] Mendieta, perhaps more than the ethnographers from whom she took her ideas of the primitive, seems to broaden this notion of performance. As with her use of Mircea Eliade's narrative, her adaptation of other anthropological stories gains force by repetition and repudiation.

Mendieta's use of this particular ethnographic narrative demonstrates her performative reinscription of it with the themes of home, nation, exile, and the land. This story involves the ritual practice of eating dirt as a means of transformation. Since the ritual of eating dirt is performed in her version of the story by women, it combines the themes of earth and the female body that are central to Mendieta's oeuvre.

It is useful to begin with the story she tells and the various versions in which it has appeared. The purpose of this is to complicate this story from the outset, to demonstrate that there is no single, original transcript to discover, that each of its manifestations betrays deep-seated ideologies that come into dialogue with each other. In a different context, Clifford explains the dizzying process of anthropological storytelling that my strategy will try to make clear: "Versions of this story, in increasing numbers, are to be heard in the folklore of ethnography. Suddenly cultural data cease to move smoothly from oral performance into descriptive writing. Now data also move from text to text, inscription becomes transcription. Both informant and researcher are readers and re-writers of a cultural invention." When considered together, all the rewritings of this tale, their alterations, gaps, and slips, work to free what Clifford calls their "extra" meanings from the bondage of scientific pedagogy.[33] As a result, one loses the sense of narrative origination, and each version becomes a repetition accumulating what Butler calls "the force of authority." One can consider the details of each version, not as data, but as the markers of different interpretative methodologies.

Although anthropologist and missionary Henri Junod was the first to publish this story in his 1912 book *The Life of a South African Tribe*, it is important to remember that even this cannot be considered the origin of the tale since, as a collector of anthropological data, Junod does not explain whether he actually witnessed the events described or was simply told of them by a native, another anthropologist, or a missionary colleague. His story may, indeed, have links to some real cultural practice, but, as soon as he attempts to capture this practice in the discourse of his science, these links are attenuated. His version, which appears only as a footnote, is as follows: "When a Ronga comes back from Kimberley having found a wife there, both bring with them a little of the earth of the place they are leaving, and the woman must eat a little of it every day in her porridge in order to accustom herself to her new abode. The earth provides the transition between the two domiciles!"[34] Anthropologist Lucien Lévy-Bruhl repeated this story word for word in his own book published in 1922.[35] From Lévy-Bruhl's version, Ana Mendieta formed her own in a statement that she wrote in the late 1970s: "There is an African custom which I think . . . is analogous to my work. . . . The men from Kimberley go outside their village to seek their brides. When a man brings his new wife home, the woman brings with her a sack of earth from her homeland and every night she eats a little bit of that earth. The earth will help her make the transition between her homeland and her new home."[36] Finally, a fourth version appears in a 1980 review of Mendieta's work by Gylbert Coker: "Like the wife in an old African folktale who was obliged to eat a little of the soil from her own homeland and that of the land of her husband in order to unite the two families, Mendieta develops a dialogue between the land and her own spirit, using the female figure to express the core relationship between the artist, the art work and nature."[37] Each of these writers engages in the production of this story; each inflects its details differently.

Junod's version, in a footnote but without being footnoted, mobilizes the language of a first-person account, complete with an exclamation point to emphasize his incredulity at the events that he himself has supposedly witnessed. Junod, a Swiss missionary in Africa, took up, for reasons both "practical and scientific," the study of the Thonga, a tribal group living in what is now Mozambique and comprising various clan groups, including the Ronga. This region had been colonized by Portugal in the sixteenth century, and Junod arrived there during the Ronga-Portuguese War of 1894–95. This particular footnote appears in the first section of his two-volume work, the first volume of which is in turn divided into two sections. The first follows an individual Ronga from birth to death, describing the various rites of passage, taboos, and rituals that he experiences. The second expands the focus to consider the customs of a kinship group. Volume 2 is likewise divided into two sections; the first considers "national life," including the "Chief, the Court, and the Army," the second agriculture, industry, and literary/artistic life.[38]

The first section of volume 1, "The Evolution of a Man from Birth to Death," actually begins before birth with pregnancy and then traces various customs of infant care. In examining the mother's diet "during the nursing period," Junod reports: "The mother herself is not allowed to drink the water of another country. She must only drink the water from home and, if she is forced to travel, she must take a little [medicine] powder from the reed each time she drinks, so that the child may become familiarized with that country." The process that Junod describes is a taboo whereby the nursing mother is required never to drink water that is not combined first with a medicine called milombyana. This medicine both enriches the mother's milk and protects the nursing child from the health hazards of the water the mother ingests. Should the child become sick, the mother, Junod reports, may give him the medicine directly by mixing it in water, which the child is given to drink.[39]

It is at this point in Junod's reportage that he footnotes the story of the brides of Kimberley. The two stories are seemingly related by the common element of eating rituals performed to familiarize the subject with another country. In the narrative surrounding nursing customs, the child is made familiar with another country by nursing from his mother, who, in turn, has drunk the foreign water purified by a special powder. In the story of the brides, they are familiarized with another country by eating porridge presumably made from the grain of the new country purified by the dirt of their homeland. For all its scientific exactitude and objectivity, this report moralizes its interpretation of the described events. Junod suggests that this practice of eating dirt is used as a means of "transition" that is ultimately meant to "accustom" the bride to her new home.

Lévy-Bruhl's deployment of this story occurs within the context of a broader examination of "primitive mentality," a comparative study of "primitive" life in various cultures and geographic locations. His primary concern is the study of mysticism, including dreams, omens, and the mystic meanings attributed to accidents and the appearance of white colonizers. He quotes Junod in the second of his chapters on "the practices of divination."

It appears that it is from this version of the story that Mendieta actually derived her own.[40] Interestingly, Lévy-Bruhl's version shows up in the context of a discussion of exile: "The man who is exiled for all time from the place where his social group has its home, ceases to be a part of it. As far as it is concerned he is dead, more really dead than if he had simply ceased to live, and had received the customary funeral rites. . . . Thus it is that permanent exile means the same thing as death." Lévy-Bruhl backs up this general claim with an example from the Solomon Islands of a man who, instead of being killed as punishment for the murder of his wife, is exiled.[41]

For him, this story and that of the brides of Kimberley demonstrate that "the location where a man may be found, the region of space in which he dwells, are 'his,' in the full sense of the word, like his limbs and his mind." Lévy-Bruhl claims that the marks left on the ground by a man's feet possess (to the primitive mind) the "characteristic quality of his personality."[42] It is clear, then, how Lévy-Bruhl transformed Junod's report from its original context in a discussion of Ronga eating taboos to its new context in a discussion of exile rituals. Moreover, he inflects the details of the story to suggest that the brides' character is derived from the dirt of their homeland.

Both Junod and Lévy-Bruhl interpret this story in terms that anthropological theorist Arnold van Gennep uses to describe the stages of ritual. These stages, which he calls *separation*, *transition*, and *incorporation*, explain a process whereby individuals pass from one state of being to another, as in, for example, marriage rites. According to van Gennep, rituals of this type are enacted in order to reinscribe and reinforce cultural norms. Yet, in the second stage of this process, the individual is momentarily undefined, occupying a liminal space between the former self and the new identity, the attainment of which is the ritual's purpose. Thus, "transition" offers a momentary disruption of the ritual's normally eufunctional role.[43]

However, Victor Turner explains that the true subversive potential of the liminal stage is only slight. He writes: "The tribal liminal, however exotic in appearance, can never be much more than a subversive flicker. It is put into the service of normativeness almost as soon as it appears."[44] Turner's interpretation of ritual as normalizing and ultimately hegemonic in this particular story is reflected in Junod's use of the contradictory words *transition* and *accustom*. Whatever disruptive possibilities inhere in the transitional phase are quickly checked by the ritual's ultimate obligation—to accustom the brides to their new home.

These two words lie at the heart of the interpretation of this story since the latter suggests a change enforced on the self, a process of making oneself familiar, of the family. There is a bitter flavor to this word, a sense of acceptance of something difficult or painful. To accustom oneself is to inure. *Transition*, on the other hand, suggests a more active, and not altogether final, process. It implies movement, a passage between states of being.

Mendieta's version of the tale employs the word *transition* when explaining the significance of the gesture of eating dirt and in so doing rewrites the tale in the very language of performance and change. In her version of the narrative, Mendieta likens the brides' experience to her own, claiming that her process of artistic creation is like their ritual of cultural mediation: "By making my image in nature I can deal with the two cultures. My earth-body sculptures are not the final stage of a ritual but a way and a means of asserting my emotional ties with nature and conceptualizing religion and culture."[45] Here, Mendieta makes a strong claim for the empowerment provided by the liminality and subversiveness of ritual. She suggests that her work parallels not its final stage, van Gennep's "incorporation" stage, in which dominant ideologies are reinscribed, but the stage of transition.

In the context of transition, the actions of the brides are performative gestures that neither reinforce their bondage nor, as in Coker's version of the story, "unite the two families." The ritual of the brides of Kimberley reflects ambivalence; it is enacted for the purpose of assimilation into a new culture, but it also reveals immutable ties with the old. Thus, it has more to do with the possibility of disrupting the process of assimilation than it has with facilitating it. That the brides perform this ritual every day suggests its inability to fix their identities permanently in their new country. Instead, they remain between two cultures, settling in the limen between the heimlich and the unheimlich.

How does the story of eating dirt help us understand Ana Mendieta's work with the earth? It seems obvious that the story's main components—women who negotiate between two countries through a ritual performance—allegorize nationhood and exile in terms of gender identity. Although the Ronga and the people of Kimberley cannot properly be considered "nations" in any contemporary sense, their interpretation as such is already begun in both Junod's and Lévy-Bruhl's discussions.[46] Junod arrived in the region now designated Mozambique in 1895, "when the age of exploration, symbolized by Livingstone and Stanley, was over, and when the age of imperial settlement and conquest, represented by Rhodes and Johnston, was begun."[47] The nationalisms that spread in Africa after the First World War had their early manifestations in the many native-European conflicts of the late nineteenth century, such as the Ronga-Portuguese War. Lévy-Bruhl expands the potential for considering the Ronga in nationalistic terms by presenting their story in the context of exile. By relating the experience of the Ronga to her own life, Mendieta makes complete its transformation.

As with her use of Mircea Eliade's primitive, her reinscription of Junod's and Lévy-Bruhl's primitive must be read in terms of the relation she drew between her own "deculturation" as a member of the Third World and that of native peoples. The stories told by Junod and Lévy-Bruhl do not, in other words, merely describe the process of exile; they are themselves accomplices in producing its mutilating effects. It is important to remind ourselves that the practice of ethnography has had a strong historical relation with colonialism and religious fundamentalism in the nineteenth century and imperialism in the twentieth. Junod's account must be read in the light of his claim that he belongs "to that body of men who, with Native Commissioners and liberal minded Colonists, feel they have a sacred duty to perform toward the weaker race."[48] The "sacred duty" to convert natives to Christianity that he so prized evolved after the Second World War into the ideology of development, in which the Third World is converted to capitalism. Mendieta appropriates the nineteenth-century account as a tool to use against its twentieth-century manifestations. The brides' experience is another version of her own.

There is more to this focus on ritual than the enactment and later mitigation of Mendieta's personal sense of exile. That she understood the story in the broader context of gender politics is demonstrated by the changes she makes to the "original" version. Whereas Junod (and subsequently Lévy-Bruhl) states that both the Ronga and his bride "bring with them a little of the earth of the place they are leaving," Mendieta writes that it is the woman alone who does so. This minor revision makes the ritual of dirt eating a specifically female activity. It casts exile more clearly in terms of gender exploitation and suggests that exile has its roots not only in political domination but in patriarchal domination as well. The bride's ritual becomes a silent protest, an enactment of the condition of the subaltern.

In this regard, the ritual affects not only those who perform it but also, and perhaps more profoundly, those who view it. The story of the brides of Kimberley helps me understand the alienation that I experience when I look at the faceless earthen body with which I began this chapter (see pl. 13 on p. 70). Like Mendieta, the brides parade their foreignness, holding tight to their bags of dirt as symbols of their exile. Perhaps the brides' dirt eating did not reassure the Ronga that their new wives would soon be assimilated. Perhaps the brides' intent was to disturb the Ronga, to make them feel homeless, to wound them with every swallow as though by the sharp points of sticks. Perhaps, as with Mendieta's sand figure, the brides' gesture made the Ronga experience the uncanny. When I think of this story, I remember that, when Mendieta returned to Cuba in 1980, she secretly brought a bag of dirt back to the United States after her visit,[49] and I imagine the beautiful brown earth of Cuba crunching between her white teeth. The sound makes me shudder.

Chapter 4

TRAVEL

It is very difficult to stay in one place when meditating on the issue of travel. To talk about travel is inevitably to engage in it, to mime through the movement of one's words that which one is trying to designate with those words. . . . [The voyage] has a powerful ability to dislodge the framework in which it is placed or understood, to subject it to critical displacement—although that displacement is not always to where one expects, nor is its criticism necessarily what one expects to find. The voyage, in other words, always takes us somewhere.
—Georges Van Den Abbeele, *Travel as Metaphor*

Henri Junod's report on the Ronga allows us to think about exile as a discursive position, to establish it as a no place to be occupied relative to permanent points of origin and destination. A Ronga journeys from his homeland (present-day Mozambique) to Kimberley, a town some five hundred miles away in (present-day) South Africa, to find a bride. The bride, taken from her homeland, travels into exile in another country. By focusing on that aspect of the story that relates to the ritual of transition between two countries, I have assumed the fixity and coherence of the two points (in this case, Mozambique and South Africa) in order to establish exile as a liminal identity positioned somewhere between them. I would like now to question that assumption because, while useful for its clarity, it is at risk of simply making exile into a third destination, a midpoint between two others. As such, exile is installed as a stable rather than a disruptive identity. My aim here will be to keep the disruptive potential of exile alive by showing that the origins and destinations around which exile defines itself are never steadfast. Each is, rather, constituted by what Bhabha calls an *internal liminality*; each is subject to the destabilizing effects of travel.

Travel is an effective concept because by definition it implies movement, it offers no rest. It keeps exile from finding a place to call its own. It is also an enormously relevant concept in that, after gaining U.S. citizenship in 1970, and before her death in 1985, Mendieta made more than eleven trips to foreign countries. In 1971, she traveled on an archaeological expedition to San Juan Teotihuacán, Mexico. In 1973, 1974, 1976, and 1978, she went with the University of Iowa Summer Multi-Media Program to Oaxaca, Mexico. In 1976, she traveled as a student around Europe. In 1980 and 1981, she returned to Cuba and, on her second visit, remained for a month to complete a series of carvings in the caves of Jaruco Park outside Havana. Finally, between 1983 and 1985, she traveled between Rome and the United States after having been awarded a fellowship at the prestigious Rome Academy.

One purpose of this chapter is to build on the efforts of the last in reimagining Mendieta's travel, not as a symptom of her loss of national identity, but as an uncanny reminder of our own. I have discussed how Ana Mendieta has been characterized as having begun her life in travel, how her flight to Miami from Cuba in 1961 stands as an originary moment for both her biography and her art. In that discussion, I argued that this first trip occupies the imaginations of critics because it marks the beginning of her exilic identity. I did not argue, however, as I will here, that it was necessary for Mendieta constantly to reinvent that identity lest it serve only to exoticize her, thereby making her exile manageable as a condition to which only she was subject.

She repeats, as do a variety of critics and historians, the idea that her work is a direct response to her expatriation from Cuba. Mendieta writes that the "insistence [on] communion with nature has to do with reaffirming my ties to my homeland" and that "having been torn from my homeland . . . during adolescence I am overwhelmed by the feeling of having been cast out of the womb (Nature)."[1] Critics, such as Gylbert

Coker, repeat these statements until they become almost clichéd. "Always concerned with being at one with nature," he writes, "Mendieta believes her works come from a deep personal experience that occurred when, as a child, she was torn from her homeland, Cuba." Other writers suggest that her work was made to "heal the wound of separation" or out of a "profound sense of displacement."[2]

The obsessive concern with Mendieta's exile appears to me to be a mask for a much deeper concern with the dangers that we all face in contemporary life as "border citizens." Beneath this focus on her dislocation lies an unspoken fear of our own. The undecidability that her travel produces makes critics anxious because it seems symptomatic of a pervasive sense of displacement, a modern condition of insecurity. John Perreault explains this idea when he writes that "the tragic sense of exile that informs [Mendieta's] artwork suggests the separateness from nature and spirit that is almost the definition of modern life."[3] He suggests that Mendieta's art is important to us, that her story of exile seems familiar to us, because it reveals how modern industrial life is incompatible with both nature and spirituality. There is more at stake here, however, to the degree that her work also makes vivid the troubling inconstancy of all those origins through which we define ourselves. These statements interest me, then, not because they provide a clear understanding of the relation between Mendieta's art and her exile, but because they exhibit both a level of experience that I believe made Mendieta aware of travel's meanings and a profound anxiety on the part of critics about travel and exile generally.

By travel, I am referring to more than simply a vacation; in this context, the word means "movement," both real and metaphoric, enacted relative to a "fixed" point and through which one recognizes oneself. That point may be a geographic location but also any established norm from which one "departs," such as gender, sexuality, or race. Ultimately, travel may reinforce a return to that norm, or it may redefine the norm to such a degree that return is impossible. I think that Mendieta was constantly forced to recognize points of national, ethnic, and gender origin and negotiate her distance from them in order either to reinforce or to redefine their normative power. As a result, she was keenly interested in how, by exploiting certain media, she could force the viewer into an awareness of the same set of negotiations. I am arguing that these media—photography, earthworks, and performance—are important, not only because their transience reflects Mendieta's own sense of dislocation, but because that transience was extremely useful in dis-locating her audience.

I have been discussing the mechanics of Mendieta's process for both securing and disrupting essential categories. Here, I would like to consider this process, not in terms of her philosophy of the earth, as I did in previous chapters, but in terms of the physical condition of the works themselves. I am proposing that Mendieta used performance, earth art, and photography precisely because, like travel, these media attempt to locate and fix representation through movement, disappearance, and dislocation. To the extent that they function within the terms of travel as I have defined it, they maintain a homologous relation with the process of identification. Capable, in other words, of producing the same kind of anxiety as the thought of exile, these media make vivid the politics of the border.

Since my argument is centered around the concept *travel* and its metaphoric implications, it is important to begin by establishing how it functions both literally and as a metaphor for identificatory practices. First of all, travel is an extraordinarily contradictory process. The mere fact of traveling from one nation to another simultaneously emphasizes and disrupts the border between them. In order to travel to a foreign country, I must first establish my citizenship; I must define myself within national borders. By crossing those borders, however, I demonstrate their elasticity. It seems that, once established in geographic terms, I carry my nationality with me irrespective of where I happen to be. In other words, nationality is first exercised in very literal terms relative to physical location but quickly becomes a metaphoric notion having little to do with material reality.

In order to metaphorize nationality in this way, the site from which travel proceeds must be produced as *home*, as an origin, an established point. An excessive romanticization of "home" (as I described in the previous chapter) helps secure that origin. It is no longer a matter of simply having been born in a certain spot on the map but one of identifying with that spot as a source of language, custom, religion, and family. As an important part of the process of identification, this "home" is no longer simply a real place but a psychological construct—a heimlich—to which is attached the susceptibility to disorientation that I have already called the unheimlich. *Home*, as a site of repression, then, always contains within itself the possibility of its own unfixing. It is itself divided by borders.

To the extent that it functions as a mechanism of control, *home* has the dual task of both safeguarding identity against the disorientation of travel and securing travel's legibility. Travel is therefore a kind of economy in which profits are calculated relative to an established value. According to Georges Van Den Abbeele, "in order to be able to have an economy of travel, some fixed point of reference must be posited. The economy of travel requires an *oikos* (the Greek for 'home' from which is derived 'economy') in relation to which any wandering can be comprehended. . . . In other words a home(land) must be posited from which one leaves on the journey and to which one hopes to return."[4] In this sense, travel is a tool by which to enforce the hegemony of the nation. One could argue, as Benedict Anderson does, for example, that travel is the means by which one determines the limits of the nation and thereby establishes it as a coherent and stable entity.

Anderson claims that the hegemony of the nation, and the ways in which it is naturalized and dehistoricized, results from an imagined sense of community that effaces difference among citizens. One might say that, for Anderson, nation is produced from the bottom up and then enforced from the top down—that it is first conceived in the minds of individuals as *home* and then governmentally enforced as homeland through language, official histories, the media, and state-run education systems. Individuals then internalize the homogeneous image of home and nation created by those in power. What links the individual conception of the nation with its official manifestations, indeed, what allows for the absorption of the former by the latter, is, according to Anderson, travel. It is through travel around the nation-space that an individual begins to view it as an entity and to subordinate his or her private interests to its public ones. Anderson writes that, in his journey, the individual learns "that his point of origin—conceived either ethnically, linguistically, or geographically—[is] of small significance. . . . Out of this pattern came that subtle, half-concealed transformation, step by step, of the colonial-state into the national-state, a transformation made possible not only by a solid continuity of personnel, but by the established skein of journey through which the state was experienced by its functionals."[5] Through these journeys, one's particular conception of the nation-space is relativized, and the nation as a self-possessed entity emerges. Anderson's theory maintains that travel discursively maps the nation-space, defining its borders and its centers.

To the extent that it functions as a source of psychological anxiety, however, *home* may also be seen as vulnerable to the indeterminacy of travel. Homi Bhabha challenges Anderson's argument by claiming that, as an ideological construct, the nation is never simply a product of state control but is also a result of individual experience, performance, and narrative. Distrusting Anderson's monodirectional representation of national hegemony (in which individuals "imagine" the nation and the state exploits their belief in it, thereafter using it hegemonically), Bhabha thinks of the nation more as a site of contestation. For him, the nation is simultaneously reinforced and undermined through individual interpretations of it, his "counternarratives of the nation." That is, *home* never achieves the fixity and clarity on which both Anderson's and Abbeele's arguments depend. Since *home* is never stable in the first place, travel merely reveals its inherent instability. It has the capacity to produce such "counternarratives" because it is unaccountable in terms of the discourse of the nation, which suggests that nations are steadfast, impervious to movement, and homogeneous. The significance of Bhabha's argument is that it provides for the possibility of subverting the nation's meanings.

The structure that I have modeled for home and travel may be adapted for the terms of other identificatory categories besides nationality. Like *nation, ethnicity, race,* and *gender* are defined by a fact of physical existence. As with *nation,* one first establishes these identities by birthright and then metaphorizes them relative to a normative standard, an essence. *Man,* for example, is predicated on biology but soon becomes an entire set of practices and attributes, the legitimacy of which is secured by the perceived stability of that biological home. As was true in the case of nationality, a "departure" from these origins can be interpreted as either reinforcing their normativity or revealing their fragility. One could, for example, examine drag as a kind of travel away from home and decide that it is profoundly disruptive to the assumed naturalness of that home or that it is only a temporary detour that ultimately reaffirms home. Indeed, this very debate has occupied a good deal of recent critical theory.[6] Moreover, this structure directly implicates the terms of representation where an image may be thought of as a home and travel the movement of the real relative to that fixed origin. Drag, passing, and upward mobility are all forms of travel enacted relative to cultural representations of sexuality, gender, race, and class.

The specific forms of representation taken by Mendieta's works are homologous with the mechanics of travel, as I have diagrammed it here. These works seem obsessively to locate and then dis-locate, to mark a spot on the earth and then depart from that marking. They posit a home, a foil, a norm against which to measure Mendieta's absence. Yet, because they are made of crumbling earth, the fleeting actions of the performing body, or photographic emulsions, the home that they construct is extraordinarily vulnerable to travel. The ontology of disappearance that characterizes these media produces anxiety in Mendieta's audience. I have never actually seen a single *Silueta,* never witnessed a single performance; relatively few people ever did. The experience that most people have of

Mendieta's works is mediated by photographs, which function something like snapshots of a lost country to which one may never return. The feelings of separation, loss, and wounding that these media encode are as disorienting as her story of expatriation.

When read as part of a narrative of travel, the Siluetas seem to have been made in accordance with a very old artistic tradition, described by Pliny in a story that I cannot help repeating:

> It was at the service of the selfsame earth that Boutades, a potter of Sikyon, discovered, with the help of his daughter, how to model portraits in clay. She was in love with a youth, and when he was leaving the country she traced the outline of the shadow which his face cast on the wall by lamplight. Her father filled in the outline with clay and made a model; this he dried and baked with the rest of his pottery, and we hear that it was preserved in the temple of the Nymphs, until Mummius overthrew Corinth.[7]

The art of portraiture, it seems, grew out of the problematics of desire and travel. The portrait occupies a point of origin, a home, produced to give meaning to the journey on which the youth embarks. It makes possible that travel; it secures an economy of movement. The distance that the youth traverses into another country measures the breach between himself and his representation. The potential to disrupt the meanings of the home he has left will be realized in this breach, the growing space of indeterminacy.

It is easy to imagine Mendieta's Siluetas as following in the legacy of the shadow traced by Boutades's daughter. Like the image of the young man drawn on the wall, these silhouettes guard against the dis-location of Mendieta's travel: they are foils against which to read the trail of her separation; they are images that firmly secure the meaning of her loss. Primarily, this is because they function as "doubles," in the Freudian sense. Almost all the works that Mendieta created were made in relation to her own body; the Siluetas in particular were initially made by tracing the outline of her body directly on the earth. Inasmuch as her works are produced indexically, and inasmuch as they refer to Mendieta herself, they appear as her uncanny doubles, which Freud describes as having connections "with reflections in mirrors, with shadows, with guardian spirits, with the belief in the soul and the fear of death."[8] The Siluetas are precisely these kinds of doubles; they are shadowy specters that leave us looking about anxiously for the person they invoke.

The shadow that Mendieta fashioned on the dirt floor of an ancient

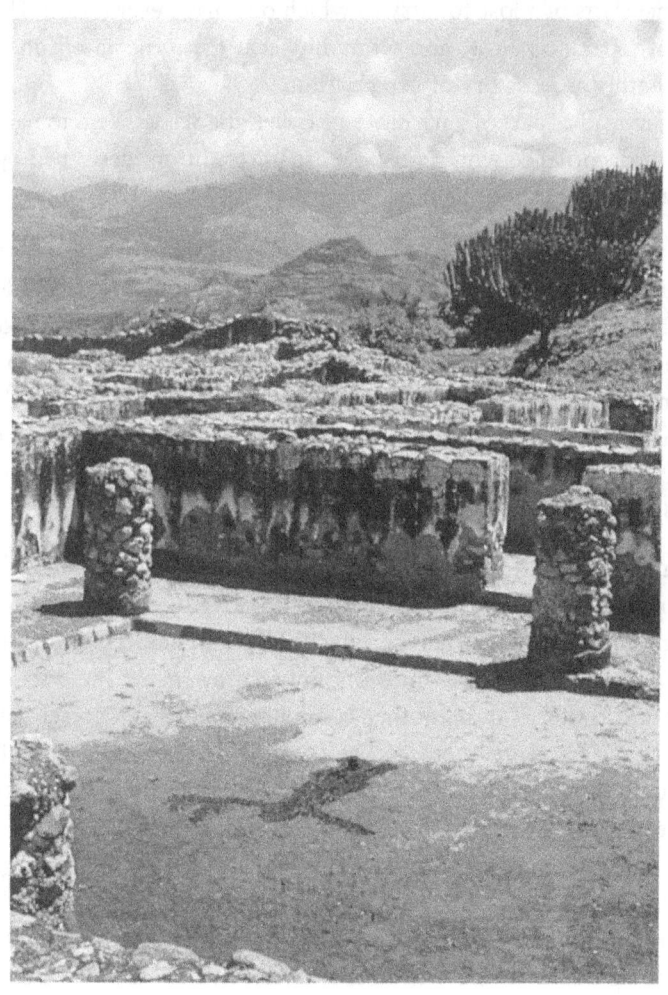

Plate 16. Ana Mendieta *Silueta de Laberinta*, 1974. Color photograph documenting earth/body work with pigment at ruins site, executed at Monte Albán, Oaxaca, Mexico, 20 × 13¼ inches, edition of twenty. Courtesy of the Estate of Ana Mendieta and Galerie Lelong, New York.

Zapotec site on a trip to Monte Albán, Mexico, in 1974, is an eerie land-mark (pl. 16). The body has been untethered from its shadow, leaving only a patch of unnatural shade in the middle of an open courtyard be-neath a bright Mexican sky. The shadow appears as though it were cast by a body overhead. An angel flying? A specter floating? A body falling to earth? This shadow is the disincarnation of the body; it marks nothing so much as Mendieta's absence. Like the shade cast by a cloud drifting over-head on a warm day, this Silueta makes me cold. In it, I feel a shiver of separation, the chill of an irredeemable breach.

As a spectral double, the shadow that Mendieta traced in the dirt at Monte Albán seems to be in some fundamental way "about" her. Like the tracing of the young man's shadow on the stone wall, it fixes her indexi-cally both in time and in place. The temptation is great, when looking at such shadows, to confuse them with Mendieta herself, to decide that they give a point of purchase on her identity. One imagines that her art is her shadow, as though, like Peter Pan's, it is sewn permanently to her feet. This conflation produces, as we saw earlier, persistent claims that Mendieta's work is made in direct response to her life, that the work is at base autobiographical. However, Mendieta is the last thing her works, as uncanny doubles, can ever be. They may allude to her presence, but they can only signify her absence; in these shadows, she is always already somewhere else. They cannot tell us who she was, only where she has been. They force us to ask, "Where is Ana Mendieta?" and to recognize ourselves in her absence.

I have argued that travel can reinforce and normalize the terms by which home is constructed and that travel is made legible by the home from which it proceeds. This effect is evident in the Silueta at Monte Albán. The shadow drawn in the dirt there marks the earth as home. As was true in the case of nationality, that home is, first, a geographic point and, second, a mythologized concept. In this case, the metaphors that circulate around earth as home involve (as I explained in the first three chapters of this book) powerful notions of the female and the primitive, the romance of life and death, and the incorruptibility of nature. These metaphors give meaning to Mendieta's journeys. She is "naturalized" as earth's citizen, and the result is that, in her travels, she always carries that home with her. The earth is as inescapable as identity itself, and travel, therefore, works only to concretize the meanings that have been established for it.

I have also argued that travel has the power to destabilize the mean-ings that are given to the home from which one embarks. This, too, is evident at Monte Albán. The origin that the Silueta establishes is extremely

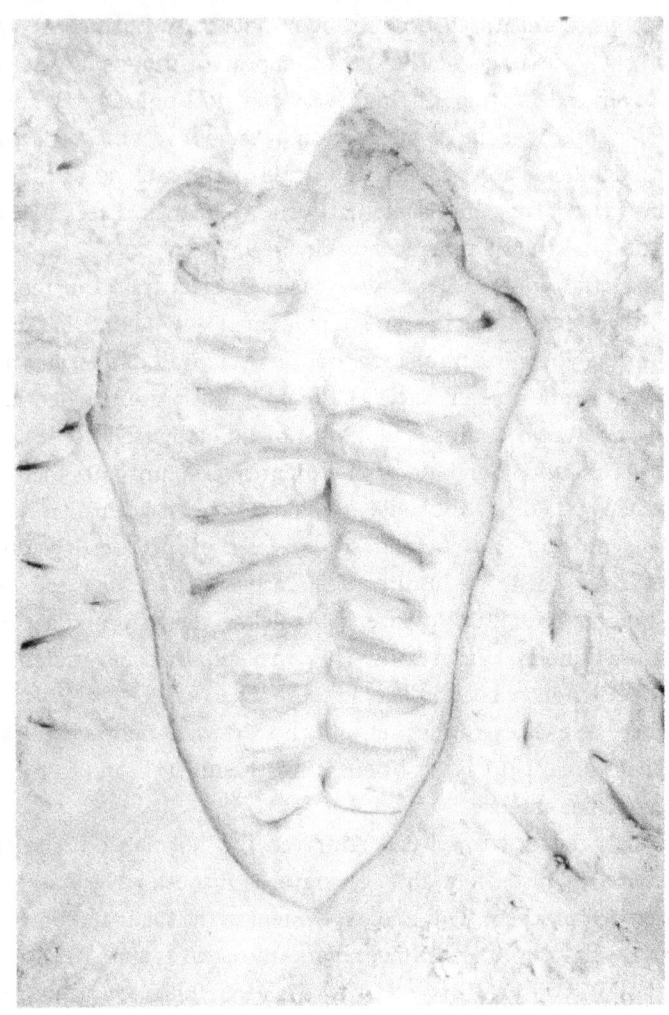

Plate 17. Ana Mendieta, *Itiba Cahubaba (Old Mother Blood)*, 1981. Rupestrian Sculptures series. Cueva del Aguila, Parque Jaruco, Havana. Courtesy of the Estate of Ana Mendieta and Galerie Lelong, New York.

fragile: it is susceptible to the slightest wind and the softest rain. As an earthwork, this piece was made precisely so that it would eventually disappear, leaving nothing tangible in its place. One might say that Mendieta first marks the earth as home, in Phelan's sense, and then unmarks it, thereby disturbing its presumed coherence. The work establishes, not just a legible site, but a breach, a troubling distance that reveals the contrivance of home through metaphor.

The effects of repair and rupture to which travel is prone are also evident in a black-and-white photograph of another of Mendieta's shadows, this time carved into the rock wall of a cave outside Havana (pl. 17). This shadow in particular is cast across the field of nationalist politics. Produced in 1981, it follows closely on Mendieta's return in 1980, after nineteen years, to her homeland. The desire to return to Cuba, about which she had spoken and critics had written, was finally satisfied. She said of her experience, "I was afraid before I went there because I felt 'here I've been living my life with this obsessive thing in my mind what if I find out it has nothing to do with me?' But the minute I got there it was the whole thing of belonging again."[9] Cutting this figure into the rocky cave wall of her homeland, Mendieta rewrites herself in Cuba; she makes it home once again.

The meanings of this carving are complicated, however, by the particular circumstances under which it was executed. When she made this work, Mendieta was a U.S. citizen; that is, in legal terms, at least, she had established the United States as her ideological home. She was forced to define her nationality in order to cross national borders; indeed, her travel to another country was considered safe only once she had done so. Here is an actual instance in which home is used to safeguard against the dangers of travel. The dangers in this case were very real to the extent that the United States has a vested interest in positioning itself politically and ideologically against Cuba. Free travel to the island threatens to muddle that distinction. Yet, when Mendieta arrived there, her original nationality, which was defined less by law than by birthright, took precedence. Her family history was entwined with the national history of Cuba; her ancestors had been the country's leaders, its rebels, its defenders. She felt that she "belonged there."

By producing the heimlich at the same time as it evokes themes of exile, solitude, and absence, Mendieta's earthen representation thereby provides a powerful discursive position from which to undermine the totalizing narrative of nationhood. In its emphatic existence within the borders of Cuba and its reference to Mendieta and her life outside these borders, this image demonstrates Bhabha's contention that "the boundary that secures the cohesive limits of the western nation may imperceptibly turn into a contentious internal liminality that provides a place from which to speak both of, and as, the minority, the exilic, the marginal, and the emergent." [10] Adapted to Mendieta's experience, this means that it is the very strength and fixity of national borders, the fact that they are heavily policed militarily and politically, that make her an exile, and it is her exile that, ironically, disrupts those borders. By producing her as an exile, the borders reveal their own fragility as psychological constructs. The contentiousness of these borders gives Mendieta a platform from which to speak. Through her work, she both claims a space, the meaning of which is inflected by nation, and escapes that space by creating a profound sense of absence. She posits woman, earth, primitive, and nation as home and then travels from it, leaving behind a meaningful breach.

The shadow that she cut into the cave wall therefore follows closely in the tradition of the shadow drawn by Boutades's daughter. It records that particular place as a point of origin against which her required return to the United States can be understood. It reinforces one national home at the expense of another, thereby both questioning the idea of nation and literally redrawing it. Cuban art historian and critic Gerardo Mosquera explains the importance of the work's site relative to nationalist history: "Inhabited long ago by the Indians, [the Escaleras de Jaruco] were later the refuge of runaway slaves and fighters in the wars of independence. In the cavern of Lost Space a field hospital functioned during the battle of 1895, and a general of the Liberation Army died there. Throughout the past history of Cuba the cliffs were a natural defense for rebels and the persecuted." [11] By choosing this site for her work, Mendieta becomes a rebel quoting a long history of Cuban resistance and reinforcing the ties between herself and the nation that she was forced to surrender.

She goes further, however, than this one border to expose Cuba's many internal borders. By making reference to the Indians forced to hide from the Creoles, the black slaves from the plantation owners, the Creoles from the Spanish, and the Communists from the capitalists, she complicates the narrative of the nation. This piece and the others she made on this site seem, thus, to rehearse the density of nationality and the profundity of its loss. They first locate and then dis-locate. Cuba was home to Mendieta, yet, to return there, she was forced to see that it was riven by time and politics. The work that she produced in Cuba is as much about the internal borders that crossed her family, her identity, and her country as it is about the national border separating the United States from Cuba.

To the degree that these works mark a boundary and then cross it, they play with the system in which home operates. They do posit a home, but one that is neither in Cuba nor in the United States, neither with nor against the family, neither in the culture nor outside it. The home that her works envision is the breach itself; what if, they seem to ask, one were at home in the border? Evidence of the liminality of Mendieta's travels may be found in her experiences of Mexico and Rome. Between 1973 and 1977, Mendieta returned every summer to Mexico to leave her shadow on the beach, on the land, or among the ruins of ancient Indian civilizations. The reasons for Mendieta's visits to Mexico were many. In one sense, her trips were the result of the fact that her teacher at the University of Iowa, Hans Breder, took his students there every summer. In another sense, it seemed that, because she could not return to her native Cuba as a result of restrictive policies begun during the Kennedy administration, she went to another Spanish-speaking country that was also rich in colonial and native traditions. It was comforting, she said, to be "where everybody was my height and had dark skin." [12] Of her experiences there, she wrote that "plugging into Mexico was like going back to the source, being able to get some magic just by being there." [13] This "magic" was manifested in the fact that, in Mexico, Mendieta did not look like the exile that she was; there, she could move easily in and enjoy a Latino culture similar to her own.

In a piece she titled *Anima*, or *Soul*, which she executed in Oaxaca in 1976, she appropriated the Mexican tradition of fireworks displays by having a bamboo armature made in the shape of her own body, attaching small fireworks to it, and setting them ablaze (pl. 18). As is common in her other works, this piece displays both the intensity and the transience of life. In it, her body, or more accurately her soul, is made of air, smoke, heat, and light. It breathes oxygen; it burns in a desirous, powerful, dangerous consumption. The work is a thrilling exultation of the body, a celebration of life's power and fragility in which the body is as intangible as light, as difficult to capture as smoke. As in a magic trick, her body appears to go up in flames that divert our attention from her disappearance. Through this sleight of hand, her corporeality and her identity are illusions. The only certainty is that she is gone.

The completely insubstantial nature of this work makes it a vivid enactment of that process of transition described in the story of the brides of Kimberley. The work is all process; it is neither bamboo armature, nor ashen remains, but a brief flame. That it was made out of a Mexican tradition, indeed, that the armature and fireworks were fabricated by

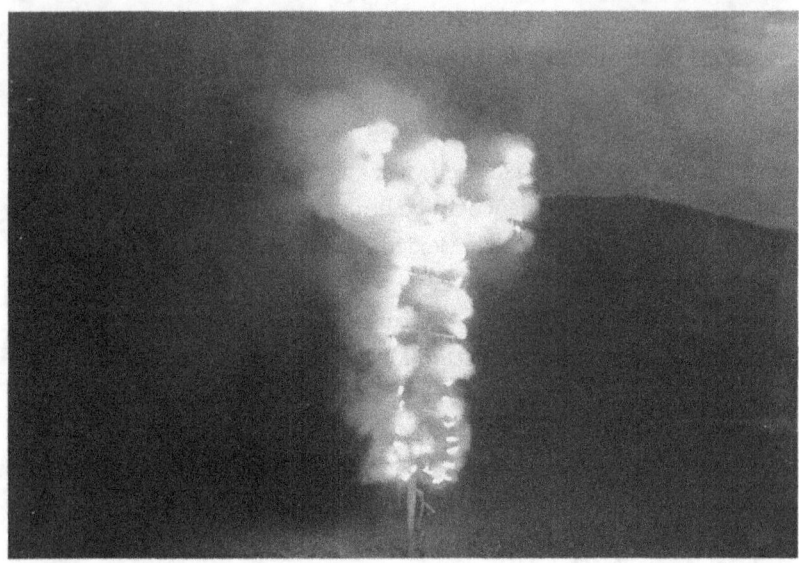

Plate 18. Ana Mendieta, *Anima (Alma/Soul)*, 1976. Unique color photograph documenting performance with fireworks and bamboo armature executed in Oaxaca, Mexico, 13 ¼ × 20 inches. Collection of Raquel Mendieta. Courtesy of the Estate of Ana Mendieta and Galerie Lelong, New York.

a Mexican *cohetero*, implicates Mexico itself as a space of transition.[14] That Mexico could constitute the site of such a transformation is a result of its unique geographic location between the United States and the Caribbean and South America. Mexico is situated as a threshold between the First and the Third Worlds. One might think of it as the borderland that separates North from South, body from shadow, home from travel. Gloria Anzaldúa explains the significance of this position when she writes that "the U.S.-Mexican border *es una herida abierta* where the Third World grates against the first and bleeds. And before a scab forms it hemorrhages again, the lifeblood of two worlds merging to form a third country—a border culture."[15] For the United States, Mexico is a domesticated Other,[16] a country that is, thanks to our interested intervention, somewhat democratic and somewhat capitalist, but not to such an extent that it is welcomed into First World status. As a result, the United States can feel safe about Mexico's close proximity and confident in growing Mexican markets while never fearing that it will be a true economic competitor. We have made certain that it functions like a buffer zone protecting the

United States from Colombia, Nicaragua, and El Salvador. This political relation had concrete effects on Mendieta's work since it made it easy to travel to Mexico. Coco Fusco suggests that Mexico was for Mendieta a "neutral territory."[17] In these terms, it seems to be not only a transitional space between two conflicting continents but also quite literally a site of passage to which Mendieta repeatedly returned.

Mexico may be envisioned as a literalization of the breach, an actual geographic gap between the United States and what it perceives as its shadowy Latin American Others. If we can think of Mexico as such a liminal space, perhaps we can glimpse the kind of power that I have been claiming for the breach. Mendieta entered this space in order to experience a cultural magic, the kind of magic that Victor Turner ascribes to the liminoid space in which "people 'play' with the elements of the familiar and defamiliarize them." Those who enter this space are, according to Turner, "temporarily undefined, beyond the normative social structure. This weakens them since they have no rights over others. But it also liberates them from structural obligations."[18] In Mexico, Mendieta is temporarily undefined: she is neither citizen nor exile. As such, she can claim no rights, but her presence there disrupts the binary terms that normally claim power over her. Mexico is not just a geographic and ideological perimeter that Mendieta crosses but a space that she simultaneously forcefully occupies and magically escapes. As Anzaldúa writes: "Alienated from her mother culture, 'alien' in the dominant culture, the woman of color does not feel safe within the inner life of her Self. Petrified, she can't respond, her face caught between los intersticios, the spaces between the different worlds she inhabits."[19] One might say that Mendieta inflates los intersticios so that they are no longer dangerous cracks into which she is in danger of plunging but vast psychological landscapes that we are invited to explore.

Another "home" that Mendieta inhabited was Rome. Her experience there in 1983 was satisfying to her in similar ways to her visits to Mexico. Raquel Mendieta suggests that "Rome was the place where she found herself."[20] Robert Katz elaborates: "Italy, for Ana, became a glorious compromise in Latinity, a midplace in the geography in her soul between Cuba and America, neither motherland nor fatherland, a kind of sisterland in which she felt strong and free."[21] Rome was for Mendieta another indeterminate space, a neither/nor territory. A plaque that now hangs at the Rome Academy makes clear the extent to which expatriation was "homely" to her. Its text was written by Raquel:

Ana Mendieta

Cuba   New York   Rome
She found her roots here.[22]

Mendieta found her roots wherever she went; she made images of home in places where she was not born and did not live. Although she was caught between Cuba, New York, and Rome, travel allowed her to empower this seemingly untenable position, to occupy militantly the interstices between worlds. In this sense, Mendieta's travel is significant neither because with it she attains a new national identity, nor even because with it she renews an old one, but instead because in travel's performance she escapes the confines of identity itself. Exile grows to such proportions that it troubles the legibility of the nations that produced it.

In my analysis, I have presumed that the images fixed by Boutades's daughter, or in the dirt at Monte Albán, or on the cave wall in Cuba, function in each instance like a home against which to read travel as either reiterative or disruptive. However, I have tried to show that the home on which these images are constructed is established as transitory, as itself a space of exile. Mendieta's works themselves, by virtue of the media in which they are executed, are not exempt from travel's ability to unsettle origins and destinations. Pliny's story has more to teach us, then, because in it Boutades takes a step that I have not as yet considered. He fills in the shadow with clay and bakes it so that it will be made permanent. It is the clay portrait that is preserved in the temple, not the drawing on the cave wall. This fact has enormous implications here, particularly if we understand the temple in Pliny's story to be a metaphor for institutional or art historical sanction. In these terms, it is incumbent on us to consider the difference between the wall drawing and the clay portrait, between media that are transitory and those that are permanent.

The two means of representation in turn require two absolutely distinct methods of historical and aesthetic analysis. The clay portrait is an object, which may be purchased, collected, preserved, and displayed. The wall drawing is temporary, site specific, and ungraspable. In this regard, Pliny's story anachronistically predicts the ideological rift that has taken place in the art world over the last half century between those artists who continue to make objects and those who make antiobjects. One can witness this rift within Mendieta's own oeuvre. Toward the end of her life (reportedly because she had not previously had a studio in which to work), she began making the counterpart to Boutades's portrait. She began experimenting

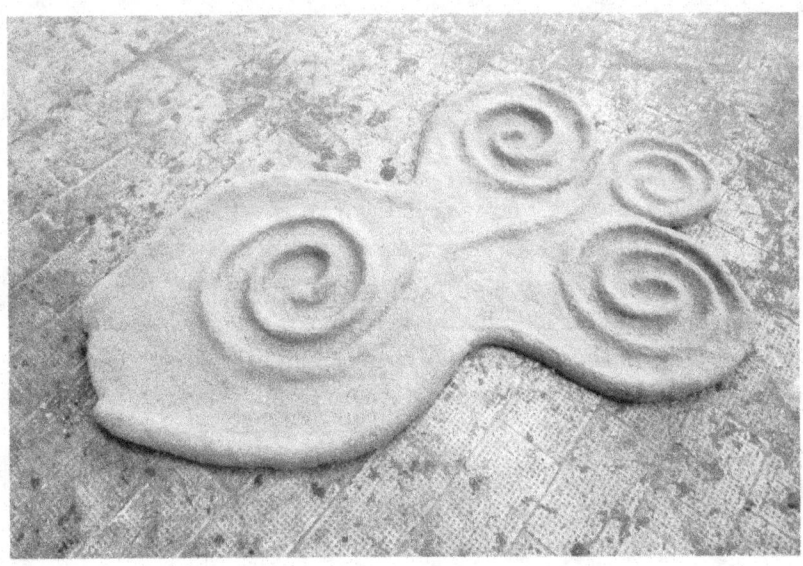

Plate 19. Ana Mendieta, untitled, 1983. Sand and binder on wood, 63 × 39 × 2 inches. Courtesy of the Estate of Ana Mendieta and Galerie Lelong.

with ways in which to fix her *Siluetas* to wooden bases using binders, the results of which are evident in a work she made in 1983 (pl. 19).

Although these works are interesting as sculptures, they have little of the dramatic emotional charge that is present in her site-specific earth works. As objects displayed indoors in presumably any gallery space, they are removed from all the meanings that they might have had in nature. They no longer refer directly to earth, nation, site, or death; instead, one is more likely to think of them in terms of their formal qualities. As a result, they are much more manageable from the point of view of art historical analysis. They fit nicely in the temple, the museum, the textbook.

By comparison, Mendieta's outdoor earthworks retain their subversive challenge to expected norms of artistic production. These works were influenced by Mendieta's familiarity with experiments in earth art, performance, video, and conceptualism. She met a variety of artists while a student at the University of Iowa, including Hans Haake, Alan Kaprow, Vito Acconci, Nam June Paik, and Willoughby Sharp.[23] Sharp, who the reader will recall wrote an essay for the catalog of the seminal exhibition "Earth Art," refers to these experiments as "impossible art."[24] Mendieta's work is "impossible" in the sense that it more closely resembles the daughter's drawing on the cave wall than the art made by Boutades. It is impossible within the regulatory terms of interpretation, which require art that is finite, tangible, and transcendent, an artist who is skillful, identifiable, and authoritative, and an audience that is kept separate from the process of creation.

I have tried to suggest how, as earthworks, these pieces embrace disappearance and dissolution, how they are contingent, traveling, and unfixed. They are, for the most part, gone. I think that it is possible to reorient ourselves to the idea that this departure is not a loss but the works' greatest strength and the source of their emotional power. These media work best in exile, the limen, the breach, the gap, the interstice, and they ask us to consider such spaces not as negative but as unmarked and therefore extremely powerful. To the extent that Mendieta's works interrogate the nature of identity, and to the extent that she understood identity to have an interstitial existence, the media in which her works are executed have a significant role in their meanings.

The chill that I feel in Mendieta's work at Monte Albán is produced by two uncanny representations: the shadow she traced in the dirt and the photograph she made of it. Each is a shadow, a spectral double of a living body. Just as the silhouette requires the once-present body, so the photograph is always tied to its referent; something must at one time have passed before the lens. The photograph names the process by which Boutades's daughter preserves her lover's image; it is a picture made by the action of light. Moreover, as with the shadow in the dirt, the fixing of the photographic image marks the absence or death of the body. "Whether or not the subject is dead," Roland Barthes writes, "every photograph is this catastrophe."[25] Barthes is referring specifically to the photographic portrait, in which the image encodes mortality: just as the fixed shadow outlives the young lover, the photograph outlives its subject. Since all photographs are shadows of something presented before the shutter's click, and since this photograph depicts a shadow in the dirt, it is, in Barthes's terms, tautological; it presents us with a redundant absence, an amplified sense of death.

The dismaying feeling of death to which Barthes refers is much like Freud's unheimlich because it is produced, not by the picturing of death (the actual representation of a dead or dying body), but through the process of doubling. Barthes senses the unheimlich, not only in photographs of himself, but in every photograph of a person, not simply because of what is presented, but because of how photography represents. Death, in Barthes's terms, is figured as absence, as loss, and one senses it in seeing a photographic shadow without a body. Like the shadow in the dirt, the photograph points to its absent double from which it has become separated. The entity that the photograph or shadow doubles is one who moves, and it is by moving that it produces a space for the viewer to consider his or her own death, his or her own loss of identity. Barthes writes that "the Photograph is the advent of myself as other: a cunning dissociation of consciousness from identity."[26] Seeing the face in the photograph is like seeing the face of the foreigner; it makes one feel " 'lost,' 'indistinct,' 'hazy.' " As shadows of shadows, Mendieta's photographic works amplify the feeling of the unheimlich, with the result that in them one feels lost, one's identity is thrown into question.

In the sense that all Mendieta's works involve an initial act of creation, the documentation of that act, and the disappearance or disintegration of its material components, it can be said that her art is fundamentally based in performance. As such, I think that it is also based on an understanding of what Peggy Phelan has called the "generative possibilities of disappearance." That is, Mendieta has a keen awareness of the potency of dissolution, absence, and intangibility. This fact places difficult demands on us as viewers; it asks us to relinquish the desire to acquire and preserve the discrete object as a thing of quantifiable value. It asks us to learn, in Phelan's words, "to value what is lost."[27] I mean (and I think that Phelan means) that we value this loss, not because we mourn it and wish that it were otherwise, but because it makes us see loss as in itself meaningful.

In this chapter, I have tried to reveal the relation between the space of loss in which Mendieta's works exist, the space of exile in which she exists, and the border that we occupy. I have suggested that to reevaluate loss and disappearance is to focus on and see the border and to realize that, while it is definitely a breach, it is not empty, that, while it is damaging, it is useful. Mendieta's work forces us to linger here. In yet another shadow, which she created in Mexico in 1976, we are brought to the water's edge and forced to confront the border, to see the trace of a body that is now no longer there (pl. 20). In this work, she inscribes her silhouette on the beach in Mexico, adds red paint to the shoal water, and photographs and films the successive stages in which the tide reclaims the figure and takes it out to sea. This shadow briefly inhabits the liminal space where land and water meet, where Mexico's national frontier begins and ends.

In the film *Fuego de Tierra*,[28] which was made after Mendieta's death, Gerardo Mosquera describes the waves in this piece as metaphorically carrying Mendieta herself back across the Gulf to Cuba. His description is dramatic because it implies more than that this work rehearses Men-

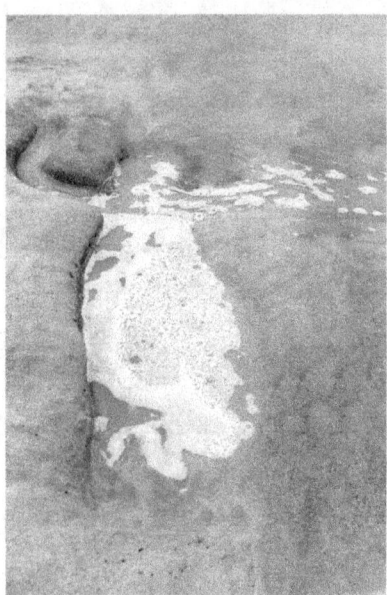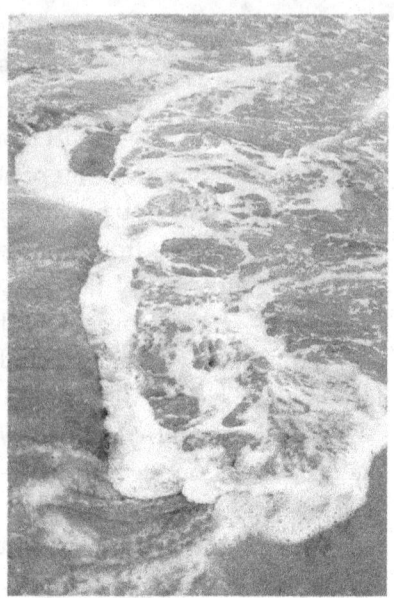

Plate 20. Ana Mendieta, untitled (*Silueta* series), 1976. Unique color photographs documenting earth/body work with sand, water and pigment, executed in Salina Cruz, Mexico, 13¼ × 20 inches. Courtesy of the Estate of Ana Mendieta and Galerie Lelong, New York.

dieta's successful return, more than that she neatly achieves a destination. It painfully demonstrates that it is impossible to make that journey while remaining whole and joyfully accepts disintegration as a means to possessing the earth. It performs the border between countries, the watery indeterminacy of identity, and the elusiveness of the body, which, like the sand, cannot be grasped. It is a map of the borderland, which Anzaldúa suggests "is a vague and undetermined place created by the emotional residue of an unnatural boundary. It is in a constant state of transition."[29]

Perhaps we should conclude this chapter thinking about Mendieta's earthen shadows as parts of a border map. It is one thing to romanticize the border, to see liminality and pretend that it is freedom. It is quite another thing to find ourselves in the border and to look at it with open eyes. The U.S. government has long toyed with the idea of digging an enormous trench between the United States and Mexico so as to deter Mexicans from crossing into "America" illegally. This image must be added to the pile of images that represent the breach between self and other, the body and its shadow. That this trench has not materialized is proof of the ambivalence maintained in the United States toward Latin America in general and Mexico in particular. While there is considerable fear about white/Latino miscegenation (both cultural and racial), U.S. industry and agriculture need the cheap labor that Latin America provides within and outside U.S. borders to produce and harvest U.S. products. They also need large markets to which these products may be sold.

Beyond this ambivalence, however, perhaps the reason that this trench has never been realized is that it is such a ridiculous image. It is ridiculous, not because of its logistic impossibility, but because of its redundancy. It would be like digging a trench where there already is one, making a border to separate us from the border. It would necessitate the digging of another trench to separate us from the first and another to separate us from the second. The trench would become a monument not only to fear and racism but also to the instability of white Western identities, a fact that becomes more obvious the more attempts are made to keep such identities pure.[30]

Another element of redundancy exists in the fact that, to a certain degree, a proliferation of trenches such as these already exists. Guillermo Gomez-Peña demonstrates this when he warns: "Today, if there is a dominant culture, it is border culture. And those who still haven't crossed a border will do it very soon."[31] Juan Flores and George Yudice reconfigure the United States in these terms when they claim that "the latest reconceptualization of America, by Latinos, is a cultural map which is all border."[32] Such a map confronts us with the tenuousness of our imagined territories; it suggests that all our fences, walls, and trenches are simply attempts to arrest the fluid movements of national identity. To map territories one must be a traveler, but to map borders one must be an exile, for it is the exile who knows that, as Gomez-Peña writes, "The border is all we share. *La frontera es lo unico que compartimos.*"[33]

Chapter 5

BODY

Color is not zero meaning; it is excess meaning. —Julia Kristeva, *Desire in Language*

The nation reveals, in its ambivalent and vacillating representation, the ethnography of its own historicity and opens up the possibility of other narratives of the people and their difference.
—Homi Bhabha, *Nation and Narration*

Ana Mendieta had a great capacity for narrative, a great interest in appropriating, telling, and redirecting stories. Her reinscription of Eliade's book and her retelling of the story of the brides of Kimberley are but two examples. This chapter takes up another, a story that brings together so much of what interested this artist and so many of her aesthetic and political strategies. In it, she plays between the binarism of essential categories, marking and unmarking the terms by which power is exercised; she travels away from origins in color and gender held fast by ideology, and she performatively redefines the terms of identity. Moreover, she uses the story directly to approach the contradictory meanings of the female body.

In 1981, Mendieta incorporated the Cuban legend of the Venus Negra

La Venus Negra, based on a Cuban legend.

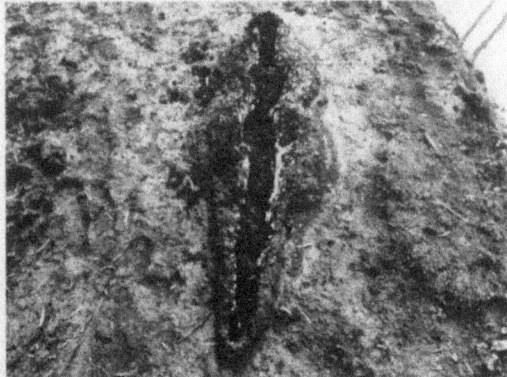

Ana Mendieta, *Silueta Series*, 1980. Earth and gunpowder.

Ana Mendieta

Around 1817, when Spanish colonists first set foot on the *Cayo Loco*—a key off the South Coast of Cuba near the city of Cienfuegos—they found a sole inhabitant. She was a young Black woman, nude except for necklace and bracelets of seeds and seashells, and so lovely that "the most demanding artist would have considered her an example of perfect feminine beauty." She was a survivor of innumerable generations of the Siboney Indians, who had been extinguished by colonization. They called her the Black Venus.

At the sight of the Spaniards, she ran—from fear rather than modesty. They caught her and discovered she was mute. Living alone on the *Cayo Loco*, she was accompanied everywhere by a white dove and a blue heron. Spreading their wings, they would touch her mouth with their beaks, in silent caress.

When one of the colonists took her home with him, gave her food and clothing, he expected her to please him and to work for him in return. But taken from her island freedom, and unable to speak, she nestled in a corner, refusing to get up, work or eat. Finally, alarmed at the prospect of her death by starvation, they took her back to the *Cayo Loco* to live in freedom.

From time to time over the years, the citizens of Cienfuegos tried again to "civilize" the Black Venus. But each time her passive protests forced them to return her to the key, where she reigned in solitude with the blue heron and the white dove her only subjects.

The historian Pedro Modesto recalled that when he was a child, around 1876, an old Black woman, with hair like a huge white powder puff and naked except for a blue, red and white necklace, secretly entered his house. She refused clothing and was dressed only by physical force. She refused all the food offered her except for native products—yucca, bananas and sweet potatoes. The next morning she had disappeared, leaving the clothes behind. That was the last time she was seen.

Today the Black Venus has become a legendary symbol against slavery. She represents the affirmation of a free and natural being who refused to be colonized.

Cuban artist Ana Mendieta has been making earth-body sculptures since 1973. She exhibits at A.I.R. Gallery in NYC and received a Guggenheim Fellowship in 1980.

Plate 21. Ana Mendieta's project for *Heresies*. Courtesy of *Heresies* and the Estate of Ana Mendieta and Galerie Lelong, New York.

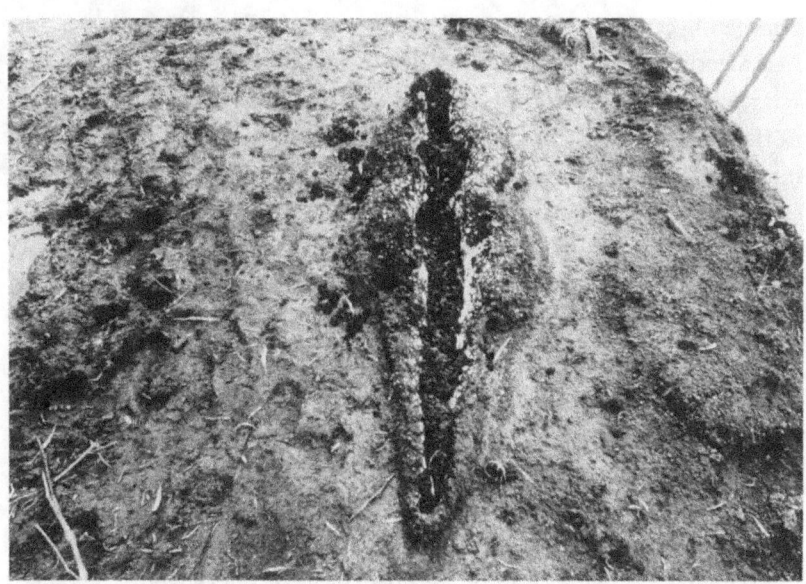

Plate 22. Ana Mendieta, untitled (*Silueta* series), 1980. Black-and-white photograph mounted on masonite documenting gunpowder *Silueta* executed outside Iowa City, Iowa, 40 × 53 inches, edition of six. Courtesy of the Estate of Ana Mendieta and Galerie Lelong, New York.

(Black Venus) into a project for the feminist art journal *Heresies* (pl. 21). Along with her translation of the story she included a photograph of one of her own works, a piece that she had executed in Iowa a year earlier (pl. 22). This earthwork is fairly typical of the gunpowder *Siluetas* she created during her career; in it, she molds the earth into an iconic female body and digs out an inner cavity, which she then fills with gunpowder and sets ablaze. This black-and-white photograph serves as the only record of the earthwork/performance. By combining this image with a hundred-year-old Cuban legend, Mendieta produces a text of great complexity, which gathers together rich and troubling elements from history, colonialism, exile, travel, and political struggle. Specifically, this work involves the ideological production of race, gender, nation, and the earth.

The meaning of the *Heresies* project's textual collage involves the strategic combination in 1981 of the photograph and the legend, which had both been created originally in other contexts. In order to approach the meanings of this project, this chapter will examine both the nineteenth-century context in which the legend was created and its later use by Mendieta. Through this examination, I want to demonstrate that both nineteenth-century Cuban Creoles (who are the legend's authors) and Ana Mendieta (the legend's translator) costume themselves as the character of the Venus Negra in order to perform their own victimization. In the case of the Creoles, since they are neither female nor black, they must stretch the meanings of gender and race in order to position themselves as victims of Spanish domination while simultaneously securing their hegemonic control of African slaves. In this costume, they reject attempts by Spain to dictate the meaning and limits of their nation-space and the nature of their agricultural economy. To do this, they liberate the body, race, and nation from essentialist meanings while at the same time appealing to an essentialist notion of the earth as a primary, unchanging, legitimizing category. Mendieta, I will argue, builds on this work by unfixing the meanings of *color* and *nation* relative to twentieth-century U.S./Cuban politics and, like the Creoles, essentializing the category *earth*. Finally, as I argued in the first chapter, I will suggest that, while similar strategies are involved in the performances of this legend, Mendieta's cannot be immediately disregarded as yet another example of a bankrupt essentialism; rather, essentialism itself must be seen as an empowering gesture in the context of her postcolonial politics. As Diana Fuss explains, "When put into practice by the dispossessed themselves, essentialism can be powerfully displacing and disruptive."[1]

Ostensibly, this is a story about a black female body, a troubling sign marked by gender and race difference. It is the story of a female Indian who resists enslavement, slips away, and haunts her potential captors. A vividly described character, the Venus Negra requires a powerful image, one that is capable of suggesting her spectral nature, her potential subversion, her elusiveness. For example, the image that Mendieta carved on the cave wall outside Havana in 1981 seems at first to answer this description (see pl. 17 on p. 100). This image, with its portrait-like orientation, crude rendering, schematic veins/bones/roots, and location in Cuba, could easily be seen as an eerie picture of the Venus. Its title, *Itiba Cahubaba*, refers, like the story of the Venus Negra, to a proto-typical Indian goddess. Itiba Cahubaba is the Taino earth mother, the first woman, the genetrix. The image that Mendieta chose to include in the *Heresies* project is, unlike the rock carving, unrelated and, in some ways irreconcilable (see pl. 22). Because of its awkward orientation (in which the ground is tipped up to meet the picture plane), it takes on an even more abstract quality than its counterpart from the cave. In addition, it depicts the anticlimax of an earthwork/performance (one that exists independently of this legend and seems to have little to do with it), and the viewer is confronted only with its ashen remains. The image relates to but cannot contain this performance, the elements of which exceed its boundaries in time and space. This limitation encodes the image with its own inadequacy to contain the performativity of its constituent themes. Ironically, it is this very inadequacy that to some degree explains Mendieta's use of the image. Although seemingly unrelated diegetically to the Venus Negra legend, in its incompleteness and lack of distinct borders this image parallels the legend's blurred history and narrative gaps. The photograph of the rock carving on the other hand, forecloses such slippage by invoking and attempting to capture Itiba Cahubaba's powers and mythical attributes. This is a story about a black female body, and, like the *Silueta* with which it appears, its efficacy is most keenly felt where it lets that body move:

Around 1817, when Spanish colonists first set foot on the Cayo Loco—a key off the South Coast of Cuba near the city of Cienfuegos—they found a sole inhabitant. She was a young Black woman nude except for necklace and bracelets of seeds and seashells, and so lovely that "the most demanding artist would have considered her an example of perfect feminine beauty." She was a survivor of innumerable generations of the Siboney Indians, who had been extinguished by colonization. They called her the Black Venus.

At the sight of the Spaniards, she ran—from fear rather than modesty. They caught her and discovered she was mute. Living alone on the Cayo Loco, she was accompanied everywhere by a white dove and a blue heron. Spreading their wings, they would touch her mouth with their beaks in silent caress.

When one of the colonists took her home with him, gave her food and clothing, he expected her to please him and to work for him in return. But taken from her island freedom, and unable to speak, she nestled in a corner, refusing to get up, work or eat. Finally, alarmed at the prospect of her death by starvation, they took her back to the Cayo Loco to live in freedom.

From time to time over the years, the citizens of Cienfuegos tried again to "civilize" the Black Venus. But each time her passive protests forced them to return her to the key, where she reigned in solitude with the blue heron and the white dove her only subjects.

The historian Pedro Modesto recalled that when he was a child, around 1876, an old Black woman, her hair like a huge white powder puff and naked except for a blue, red and white necklace, secretly entered his house. She refused clothing and was dressed only by physical force. She refused all food offered her except for native products — yucca, bananas and sweet potatoes. The next morning she had disappeared, leaving the clothes behind. That was the last time she was seen.

Today the Black Venus has become a legendary symbol against slavery. She represents the affirmation of a free and natural being who refused to be colonized.[2]

In this fable, Cuban Creoles fantasize about a meeting in which Spanish colonists have one last glimpse at the Siboney Indians, who had in reality vanished long before 1817. By telling this story, the Creoles dissociate themselves from their Spanish ancestors and think romantically about the bravery of a race of people in whose genocide they are accomplices.[3] Therefore, the legend is historical only in the sense that it serves as a marker for a gap in the collective memory of the conquering race. The Venus is clearly a figment of the colonial imagination. An ambiguous historicity controls the power of her brazen black body.

One of the peculiarities of this tale is that, despite its status as legend, it employs the discourses of history and anthropology in order to signify the "real"; its efficacy depends both on a rhetoric of fact and on a discourse of origins. It seems on one level to be referring to a historical personage whose existence has been documented by scholars (Pedro Modesto) and whose appearance can be traced to a specific date (1817) and a real place (Cienfuegos). As much as this rhetorical strategy works to naturalize the story of the Venus Negra, there remains a fictional element that is at odds with the tale's production of a palpable reality and that undermines its ostensible theme of Indian resistance. This element is most clear when the story is considered in the light of other stories of colonization, which do not end so happily. One wonders in particular why, given the Spanish colonists' decided lack of squeamishness at the sight of other people's blood, they did not simply kill the Venus Negra rather than return her to her home. That she is spared suggests that the Venus Negra is always already a sign; she is not a person to get away or be killed but a rare image. This is emphasized when in the legend we are told that she is so lovely that "the most demanding artist would have considered her an example of perfect feminine beauty." She is not only the Venus of Greek myth but the Venus whose name sanctions an extensive history of European artistic production of the idealized nude. In order not to die, she must be extraordinarily beautiful; in order to be a sign, her black body must be turned into a vision.

The uses to which this vision has been put are of considerable importance to us here, for this is not really an antislavery success story. The fact is that this fable did not serve a native identity or the politics of insurgency among Indians. Rather, it provided a source for the formulation of nascent Cuban Creole identity, an identity that had to be formed in contradistinction to that of the European Spanish during the nineteenth-century struggle for Cuban independence.[4] The story thus became a part of the nineteenth-century discourse promoting Cuban protest against the colonial domination of Spain.[5] Cuba was the last country in Latin America held by Spain. The successive uprisings, beginning in 1819 and occurring periodically until the Cuban war of independence, came in response to stringent colonial policies and to Spain's mismanagement of Cuba's economic resources. Despite the great profits that their sugar and tobacco crops meant for the peninsular Spanish, the Creoles were heavily taxed but could not occupy public posts, set up independent industries, or have any rights to legal action against Spaniards.[6] In this story, the white Creole clothes himself in the black female Indian body in order to perform the threat of victimization posed by the Spanish. But why this costume? Why has the Creole chosen the black female body as the vehicle for resistance, and what specifically are the goals that such a strategy might hope to achieve?

The Venus Negra narrative contributes to the nation's performativity, and it is an attempt to reformulate the means by which the nation was imagined. It does this, I believe, by claiming a precolonial, prediscursive deed to the land that supersedes any claim by the Spanish. The story functions as another "counternarrative of the nation," in which an appeal is made to an essentialist notion of the land, as a more natural and primary category, in order to de-essentialize the nation, the earth's secondary and culturally determined identity. The Venus Negra signifies the natural inhabitant of the island whose more legitimate claim to the land is threatened when she is unjustly captured by foreign colonists. As such, she rehearses the escape from foreign control that Cuban Creoles would later enact in their revolution of 1898. Their right to self-determination is legitimized through a narrative strategy in which one essentialist category trumps another. The Creoles are the closest thing to "natives" on the island, so their claim to its wealth of natural resources is stronger than that of the Spanish colonizers.

It is important to see that the happy ending that the legend promises depends, first, on the strict division between *earth* and *nation* and, second, on the alignment of *female* and *black* with *earth*, all three of which fall under the heading *the dispossessed* (a move that I have already discussed). Through this narrative linkage, the "artificial internal coherence," to use Judith Butler's phrase, of gender and color is disturbed so that white males can clothe themselves in a black female body. This "drag" performance causes me to wonder along with Butler, "Is drag the imitation of gender, or does it dramatize the signifying gestures through which gender itself is established?"[7] In other words, as a form of travel from home, does drag reinforce a return to that home or a redefinition that makes return impossible? If the latter is the case, then, in choosing a black female as the incarnation of their own victimization, Creoles risk empowering the other (and arguably "real") victims—women, blacks, and Indians— in whose masks they perform their own independence. As a result, this narrative both deploys and attempts to control the subversive potential of gender and color.[8]

The value of the Venus Negra costume is that, when dressed in it, one automatically moves closer to the earth, to nature itself. One becomes a native with a preordained right to the land, a right that was inconceivable in the period of exploration but took on more rhetorical force in the nineteenth century when the original "natives" had been largely eliminated and the stakes in claiming territory grew. That the Venus is aligned with the earth is due in part to her gender; the long tradition associating the female body with the earth culminates in sixteenth- and seventeenth-century representations of the "New World" personified by the nude female body. In such representations, the female body signifies both untouched beauty and sexual availability, both an admiration for nature and a desire to tame it in the service of expansionism. The kind of ambivalence that surrounds this traditional association finds its way into the legend of the Venus Negra.

The Venus is presented as though she were a naturalist's curio—the sole example of her kind. She is a rare and coveted specimen whose place in the explorer's notebook is secured by her gender and race difference, which defines her for the colonists as an object of loathing, as a sexually available object, and as a low other whose kinsmen were slain with trifling ease and little remorse. But, at the same time, she is a rare beauty to be admired, collected, and preserved.[9] This paradoxical perception of the Indian body has an extensive pedigree stretching back to the time when Columbus first stepped onto the shores of this largest of the Caribbean islands. Columbus's diary is filled with careful notes on all strange new flora and fauna, in which are included representative examples of the Indians he meets. The Indian woman inscribed there is like a beautiful parrot, a tall palm tree, an animal of unknown species, a beautiful, tropical, wild, primitive being of considerable interest to the explorer. But she is also simultaneously an object to be collected, used, and destroyed. The travel accounts of early explorers are similarly replete with descriptions of the sexual use of the female Indian body, of frequent and brutal rapes that would never have been considered as such, and atrocious murders no more criminal than the hunting of wild animals.[10]

Within this tradition, the Venus Negra is a figure of huge ambivalence. She at once assumes a definitively "low" position and a small measure of power, the only kind of power available to such a creature—her naturalness itself. By refusing to yield to the trappings of civilization, she reclaims herself as untractable and becomes that most noble of animals that one simply must return to the wild. Unlike so many of her kindred, she is not raped or murdered but returned to her home in what seems at first to be an unprecedented victory. However, she is no more free there than if she were on zoological display, for her life has been spared so that she can serve as the signifier of an ever-diminishing wilderness. She is a curiosity, the last of a species not far from extinction, and as such she symbolizes both the power of those who have accomplished this elimination and the nostalgic feelings about what has now been safely lost. Her travel away from and return to this "home" helps secure its meaning as "nature to be preserved," presumably by the Creoles.

The Venus is quite literally associated with the land that she occupied, so much so that it is feared that she will die if she is not returned to it. As a personification of the earth, her acts of resistance may be characterized as a refusal to participate in an economy of agricultural exploitation. The refusal to eat anything "except for native products—yucca, bananas and sweet potatoes" seems to be a reference to the particular history of Spanish exploitation of Cuban land. Cuba's ability to produce and trade in native products was destroyed by the planting of vast acres of sugarcane, which is not a native plant, and which brought food and profit, not to native Cubans, but instead to colonials back in Europe. In addition, sugar and other colonial crops, which Eduardo Galeano (following José Martí) refers to as "monocultures," destroyed the ecological balance of the island, robbing the soil of essential nutrients, and placing the landscape at the mercy of the vagaries of the European markets.[11]

In the light of the history of Cuban agrarian practice, the Venus's insistence on native foods seems in a larger sense to resist that aspect of colonization that is driven to exploit the land for profit. In this regard, the black body of the Venus takes on particular significance. The darkness of her skin becomes analogous to the darkness of the earth; her body is a metaphor for the Cuban soil before colonization, a landscape that was still fed only by native plants. This part of the legend urges a return to native agricultural production, to self-determination among the Creole population. By their association with the Venus Negra, both the land and the Creoles are cast as victims of colonial intervention. This story depends on a rhetoric of "first claims" to challenge the legitimacy of foreign control.

That she will not dress or work suggests that the Venus Negra will not engage in trade with the colonists. There is an expectation on the colonist's part that, if he feeds and clothes her, she will "please him and . . . work for him in return." He means to trade food and clothing for labor and sex. In this miniature economy, the body of the Venus is the key to exchange; its clothing, nourishment, and ability to labor and sexually satisfy are the coins of the colonial market. What secures the value of her body is primarily that it is female but also that it is black. To the extent that the Venus Negra refuses to dress, her blatant blackness becomes an image of itself. In her refusal, she tactically insists on her gender and color difference; she insists on being other. The colonists' attempts to clothe her are not driven so much by morality and shame as they are by the need to cover and neutralize her difference in a strategy of assimilation. The body of the Venus Negra is a constant reminder of what lies just beyond the parameters of "civilization," just beyond the system of colonial control. Like some uncomfortable vestment, the Creoles wear their Spanish heritage and wait for a time when they can re-dress themselves in the costume of self-determination. Meanwhile, the Venus Negra's body embodies blackness, proclaims color, will not hide gender, is a picture for desire and loathing.

When Judith Butler writes that "gender is performatively produced,"[12] she, like many other cultural theorists, liberates gender from its hegemonically constructed binarism. While the legend of the Venus Negra and its use by Cuban Creoles certainly demonstrate Butler's claim, I would like to add the possibility that color is also "performatively produced." The verity of this idea may be seen most obviously in the notion of *passing*, in which one attempts to present oneself as a member of a race or group to which one does not customarily belong.[13] While *passing* may not always refer to an actual physical passage or movement, I would like to consider it as such, to see it as a result of the performativity of color, and in turn to see it as a site of subversion. In their use of the Venus Negra legend to challenge the limits of their proscribed nationality in particular, the Creoles seem to be critically and subversively "passing" for black.

In order to view passing as a subversive performance in the specific context of this legend, it is necessary to outline the ways that color is related to movement. First, it is through travel or exploration that groups take on color; second, geographic regions are themselves associated with particular colors; and, third, one's color can change through travel from one location to another. Moreover, like other identity categories, color functions within the terms of travel. That is, it is first defined biologically but thereafter takes on metaphoric and ideological associations. It is established relative to a "home," a normative standard, the departure from which is potentially troubling.

It is clear in this legend that the movements of Europeans to the Western Hemisphere have literally produced an encounter with other colors, that the whiteness of the colonists takes on a value as white only in relation to those other colors against which it is viewed. The colonists stumble through the dense foliage of an undeveloped part of the island to discover the blackness of the Venus Negra. Indeed, in this story, she is blackness itself, and, although it is never explicitly stated, the colonists are white. Their travel from Europe to Cuba makes possible this encounter in which their own color is defined against that of the native Indian. This process of color definition hints at the real possibility of the Venus's subversiveness because, as Richard Dyer writes, the power of whiteness is secured by "making it hard . . . to see whiteness." [14] In this chance meeting in the forest, color takes on a distinct clarity. The colonists become white in the presence of the Venus Negra, and their source of power is unmasked. The Creoles, whose pale skin might otherwise signify the ancestry that they share with the colonists, dress up in a darker skin in order to perform their role as the victims of colonial aggression.

Beyond the obvious fact that whites from Europe became white only when they encountered other races with distinctly different skin colors, there is another way in which we might say that color is related to movement; that is, color is often associated with geographic location. Tzvetan Todorov provides an example of this when he explains that, in his need to find gold and other riches, Columbus used both natural phenomena and native bodies as tools of divination. In Columbus's journals, "blacks and parrots are . . . considered as the signs (the proofs) of heat, and heat as the sign of wealth. It is hardly surprising then that Columbus never fails to remark the abundance of parrots, the blackness of skins, and the intensity of the heat." [15] In this example, there is a conflation of natural, geographic phenomena and the color of the inhabitants of a particular region. The Creoles appropriate this conflation to their own ends. They associate themselves with the specific geography of Cuba in order to claim natural ownership of it.

In addition to geography's relation to color, land itself and one's association with it seem to be implicated in color definition. Here, the color of the earth is aligned with the color of those who work on it. For example, Eduardo Galeano describes the results of the fact that peasant farmers from a small village in Argentina have been forced to leave their farms for a chance at a better life in Buenos Aires: "A few years ago sociologists asked the one hundred and fifty survivors of a La Rioja village if they saw any change in their former neighbors who had left and returned on visits. Those who had remained said enviously that yes, Buenos Aires had improved the emigrants' clothing, manners, and way of speaking. Some also found the emigrants to be 'whiter.'"[16] In this anecdote, it becomes clear that dark skin is related to the countryside, farming, and working with the soil, whereas light skin is associated with the city and all the "civilization" that it symbolizes.

Moreover, this story indicates the third significant aspect of color's performativity: color becomes visible through travel, color is related to particular types of geography, and now, most significantly, color can be changed as a person moves closer to or further away from geographic locations like city and country. The implications of color's instability are provocative since they mean that color is an elusive category, that it can be used as a tool of social mobility. Through movement, color achieves a liminal quality. Through its performativity, one can pass—in both the sense of getting away with something and that of passing from one state of being to another. Creoles pass for black in order to strengthen their associations with the earth, in this case meaning the land or soil of Cuba, which in turn allows them to legitimize their narrative of nationhood and to challenge the story that the Spanish have produced for them.

But this analysis comes nowhere close to exhausting the use of color as a signifier in the story of the Venus Negra. That she is black and not brown is another complex issue since, although black is used to describe the native, it must also refer to the African slave population in Cuba, which was at this time considerable. How can the Venus be black but not African? Why is she chosen as the one to get away when the successful liberation of a black slave might represent the subversion of colonial authority with more urgency?

By 1817, Cuba had already been thoroughly colonized, and large cities had grown up around the island, which were key centers for the transportation of goods from Mexico and South America to Europe. Interestingly, black slaves had been introduced to the island with the first conquistadors, and, by the middle of the nineteenth century, their population exceeded that of whites.[17] What makes the encounter with another black body so significant, then? I believe that it has to do on one level with the blatant nakedness of this body and the rejection of European civilization that the refusal of clothes symbolizes. This black body, found in the remote countryside, wears instead the signs of its excess. It presumes to be natural, rural, uncivilized, the very color of the earth. It is itself a sign of a crack in the colonial enterprise, a body and a region that have escaped "civilization."

On another level, however, the significance of this encounter with a black body results from the fact that it is not the same as the black bodies of the African slaves who had been forced to travel to the colony from afar. Theirs is a blackness that signifies foreignness, hers a blackness that signifies nativeness. In other words, her blackness marks her relation with the earth; it allows her to claim an original deed to a very valuable plot of land. The blackness of the slaves allows them to claim nothing.

In addition, theirs is a blackness that was much more problematic in the context of the struggling colony. In very basic terms, although the Creole population was negotiating its independence from Spain, many Creoles feared severing all ties with Europe because they worried that, without Spanish intervention, there would be uncontrollable slave uprisings. Since their own prosperity (as a relative minority) depended on the brutal exploitation of blacks and mulattoes (who were in the majority), it was of primary concern to maintain the machinations of slavery. They traded their independence for economic prosperity, while Spain persisted in stacking the deck in its own favor by continuing illegally to import slaves to the island, with the aim of outnumbering white bodies with black ones. In this situation, the black African body served as a constant reminder of the Creoles' concession to Spain. "In the face of every slave," Robert Paquette writes, "Creoles could see a mirror image of their own colonial servility."[18]

It is clear, then, that the symbol of subversion of colonialism had to be chosen carefully; color had to be black, but not that black. It had to be a blackness in which Creoles could feel pride and not fear, in which they could see themselves as powerful and not as just another kind of slave. Clothed in this particular shade—while dressed in a costume only tangentially resembling that of their most immediate victims—they could perform their own victimization. This shade had to be a blackness that no longer existed, a blackness that was more of history than of skin.

I have already discussed to a certain extent the meanings that this story was meant to have, the ways in which it suggests subversion while keeping it always under control. What I have hinted at, and what I now would like to discuss more directly, is the fact that I do see the Venus Negra as a subversive figure in that she utterly confounds the understanding of color and gender. Despite their best intentions, the unknown authors of this story have had, in order to achieve certain national and colonial goals, to make identity categories slippery. In their performance, the repetition of the narrative is empowered by the historicity of its elements. Despite the fact that it is a repetition, however, it is not a duplication—the performance, to a certain degree, turns against history. Like the Venus Negra, color and gender have gotten away from them.

By employing this narrative in her project, Mendieta exploits this slipperiness to produce a work of bewildering complexity in which the meanings of *gender, race,* and *nation* are by turns fixed and disrupted, then imbricated to such an extent that it is difficult to discuss them as separate entities. She essentializes the categories *woman, color,* and *earth* and then, through her earthworks, "dresses up" as the Venus Negra to perform exile and thereby produce a counternarrative of the nation. Although her strategy, of unbaptizing or unmarking essential categories, is persistently problematic, it carries great rhetorical force.

Mendieta's use of the Venus Negra legend relies, as do many of the other examples that I have discussed, on an essentialist understanding of gender and color. For Mendieta, the Venus Negra stands for a kind of primitivism to which she herself felt a kinship. It is worth repeating the statement that I quoted earlier on this subject: "It is perhaps during my childhood in Cuba that I first became fascinated by primitive art and cultures. It seems as if these cultures are provided with an inner knowledge, a closeness to natural resources. And it is this knowledge which gives reality to the images they have created." [19] Here, Mendieta herself seems to betray, in language only slightly different from that of the Spanish conquistadors, a belief that I have already discussed—the allegorical relation between the darkness of the earth and the darkness of the skin. By appealing to this trope, Mendieta risks producing a rhetoric informed by a tone of condescension and nostalgia of which anthropologists, like colonialists, have been all too guilty. However, her problematic use of this story is made more complex by and in response to feminism.

On the one hand, Mendieta pursues a strategy common to feminists of the late 1970s and early 1980s; that is, she attempts to see change in the future by searching for origins in the past that demonstrate the possibilities for women to break out of their prescribed roles. Through a strategy of passive resistance, the Venus Negra challenges her male captors and wins her freedom. This emancipation rehearses the liberation of women that feminism attempts to enact. In short, Mendieta uses anthropological methods to define alternatives to the condition of women in her own time. This work casts the Venus in two roles; she plays both a real Siboney Indian and Ana Mendieta herself. As Michelle Rosaldo has so insightfully explained: "By using anthropology as precedent for modern arguments and claims, the 'primitive' emerges in accounts like these as the bearer of primordial human need. Women elsewhere are, it seems, the image of ourselves undressed, and the historical specificity of their lives and of our own becomes obscured. Their strengths prove that we can be strong."[20] The strengths that this story is meant to prove include, not those of women generally, but those of women of color specifically. Mendieta engages the story's "primitivism" as a critique of feminism's racial bias. Despite her decidedly white European heritage, as an artist in the United States Mendieta was not white; indeed, she was consigned to and accepted that amorphous identity of the nonwhite. This identity is ill defined because, in the United States, there is no room for the epistemological complexities of color and race in Latin America (or anywhere else for that matter), and, as a result, we tend to describe people of widely divergent national, ethnic, and racial backgrounds with radical imprecision.[21]

Since she is white *and* Cuban, a U.S. citizen *and* an exile from a Third World country, Mendieta has neither a clearly defined color nor a clearly enunciated nationhood. I have already described the sense of disempowerment attached to the ambiguity of this position and how it prompted her to write that the goal of women artists of color was to "continue being 'other.'"[22] In this statement, Mendieta invokes a stance remarkably similar to the one taken by the Venus Negra, who also seems driven by a "personal will to continue being 'other.'" She expresses a desire, not for inclusion, which would mean racial and cultural assimilation, but for difference. She affirms instead the performative power of exile. It would appear that Mendieta performed this exilic identity by embracing the color that racism had assigned her. Instead of passing for white, Mendieta was passing for black, a blackness that she understood through her own experience to be elusive, marginal, and uncontainable.

Roberto Fernández Retamar explains the impetus for Cubans of white

European ancestry to align themselves with native Indians and slaves—in a sense, to become black. The epithet *mambí*, Retamar writes, "was disparagingly imposed on us by our enemies at the time of the war of independence. . . . To offend us they call us *mambí*, they call us *black*; but we reclaim as a mark of glory the honor of considering ourselves descendants of the *mambí*, descendants of the rebel, runaway, *independentista*, black—*never* descendants of the slave holder."[23] This mutability of color is essential to what the Cuban writer José Martí would call "our mestizo America," an America in which identities are marked by hybridity.[24] Martí makes it clear, however, that *mestizo* means not solely a mixture of blood, a child born of parents of different races, but also the irrevocable mixture of cultures that lies at the heart of Latin American history. *Mestizo* is as much a historical as a biological quality. In addition to skin color, it suggests race, ethnicity, heritage, and class and thereby proves, not the possibility of naming color, but its impossibility.

Therefore, Mendieta's choice to associate herself with the Venus Negra, with the native Indian, is a typical strategy by which Latinos define their identities relative to the problematics of race, politics, and nationhood. In this strategy, one aligns oneself with the black slave or *el indio*, those who most dramatically symbolize the victimization perpetuated by groups that one opposes. It is another example of Mendieta decrying her own "deculturation" as a Cuban exile by comparing it to the "deculturation" of native peoples at the hands of their colonizers. It might be helpful here to remind ourselves of her claim that "in the past as well as in our own century in order to facilitate the expropriation of the natural richness of a territory and/or use the people as labor, the process which has been and still is very much implemented is DECULTURATION. Its purpose being to uproot the culture of the people to be exploited." The Venus Negra is a symbol of both colonialism and neocolonialism. Mendieta's use of this symbol insists on the liminal nature of color, a purposeful confusing and mixing of the iconography inherent in the skin. It questions what color is, how it relates to race, how it signifies in a cultural economy of privilege and exploitation.

Just as Cuban Creoles essentialized the notion of earth in relation to their island, giving it a primary signification that deconstructs the imagined nation, so Mendieta employs an essentialized notion of the earth to problematize the meanings of the nation in her own era. Yet there is a significant distinction between these deployments of the category *earth*. The Creoles' notion of earth relates to the soil or land of their country. It is, thus, coterminous with the island's borders. Mendieta's notion of earth is, as has been said, *the* earth, an earth that is coterminous with the globe and therefore one that exceeds all national boundaries.

In expanding the horizons of her referent, Mendieta engages the politics of color, gender, nation, and race with issues of broad-scale environmentalism. Mendieta's *Heresies* project is included in an issue on ecology, the theme of which may be summarized by another contributor: "Nature feminists repeatedly remind us that we are part of the earth and the universe, part of a great interdependent community of both animate and inanimate beings."[25] The trope of the "great interdependent community" to which the ecology movement must constantly refer is problematic for the narrative of nation, which depends, according to Bhabha, on ideas of "progress, homogeneity, cultural organicism," and deep national history.[26] In these terms, the notion of the earth depends on our ability to imagine its singularity of meaning and our ability to see it in contrast to the divisive multiplicity of nations.

The earth, bounded only by its astronomical proportions, exposes the contentious, shifting, imaginary boundaries of the nations that attempt to divide it. Mendieta's performance, in which the earth burns with volcanic power, and her photographic remnant, in which there is no longer room to see a horizon, reveal the rhetorical power of such a global focus. As a result, this *Silueta* is a potent enactment of reclamation for those who are victimized by the ideology of the nation. The Venus is a paradigmatic border citizen, a legendary figure who refuses to be colonized by language, dress, custom, the sword, or the gaze. By her refusal, the colonists are undone. Mendieta's project stacks up the elusive *indio*, the incorruptible female body, the shifting nation, and the unbaptized earth. Igniting the pyre, she leaves us waiting to sift through the ashes with blackened hands, fearful of touching hot coals.

Conclusion

WRITING TOWARD DISAPPEARANCE

Performance resists the balanced circulation of finance. It saves nothing; it only spends.
—Peggy Phelan, *Unmarked*

For me, Ana Mendieta is an artist who is herself "unbaptized," in the sense that she and her work are as yet unclaimed by historical discourse. In imagining her thus, I find myself in the contradictory position of wanting to save her both through history and from history. My task has been to produce a narrative for her, to legitimize her work, to claim a space for her in the art historical canon. It has been to answer the question, "Where?" Yet I know that the answer may not satisfy, that it is wrong to argue "that communities of the hitherto under-represented will be made stronger if representational economies reflect and see them."[1] The urge to locate Mendieta dangerously assumes that securing a place in the history of art necessarily translates into increased power, an assumption to which many women and artists of color have fallen victim. So, at the same time that I have tried to historicize her, my work has tried to protect her from the sometimes stifling, limiting effects of historical discourse. Thus,

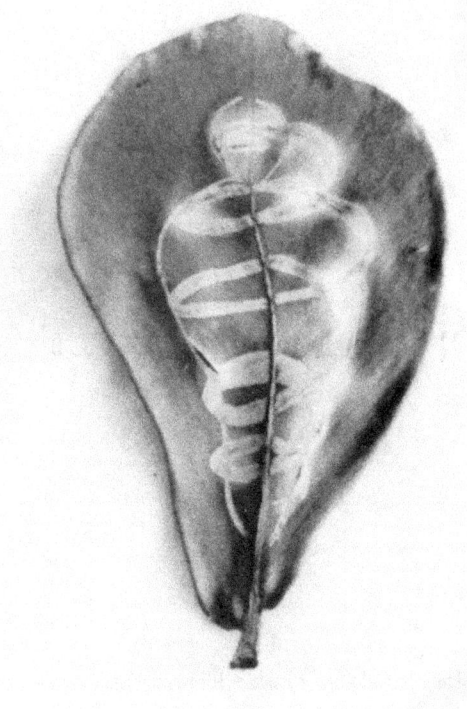

Plate 23. Ana Mendieta, untitled, 1982–84. Drawing on leaf, 6 inches. Courtesy of the Estate of Ana Mendieta and Galerie Lelong, New York.

I am led into paradox. If I admit that marking/baptizing/writing Mendieta cannot save her (in a redemptive sense), do I not at the same time save her (in a protective sense) from any discourse but my own?

I was reminded of this dilemma when I first saw, at Galerie Lelong in New York, one of the drawings that Mendieta did directly on leaves (pl. 23). This tiny work was brought to me in a small box in which it rested on tissue paper as though it were a gift. The leaf, brown and dried, was inscribed with an abstract drawing of a female figure whose curving spine was formed by the leaf's central vein. The drawing, breathtakingly beautiful in its absolute fragility, did not affect me as much as the box in which it was stored. The box made Mendieta's tiny artwork seem like a child's treasure, preserved in some cast-off jewelry or glove box, packed in cotton or tissue. Holding the box in my hands, I was struck by the thought that I could quite easily crush the leaf to dust, an act that I could never perform but the thought of which haunted me. To destroy the leaf seemed to me an act of inconceivable brutality, as though it meant physically harming another person.

What could account for this hysterical fear? What kept me from crushing the leaf? The box did; it marked the leaf as precious, as an object to be saved. In the box I began to see the act of historical preservation through writing. Writing history about work like Mendieta's was like keeping a dead leaf in a box under your bed; it was like saving something that had already been lost. Had I pulverized the leaf, in other words, it would have been more threatening to history, more destructive to me, than it would have been to the leaf itself. What would a history look like, I wondered, that took the death in Mendieta's works seriously? What kind of history is it that does not save?

This question makes clear to me the fact that one of the greatest achievements of Mendieta's art is that it perplexes historiography. I mean, not that her work is absolutely unprecedented and therefore requires some utterly new model of explication, but that it (along with a great deal of the art of the last three decades) asks history writing to do something that by definition it cannot do. That is, it asks history to let go of the past. In addition to everything else that I have said about it, this work shows extraordinarily clearly the disappearance that we must learn to celebrate — the disappearance of her work, of our grasp on categories that we thought were pure, of ourselves from the terms of cultural legibility. It challenges us to come up with new methods of critical and historical analysis that are not self-deluding, that are "primitive" in the sense that they preserve the past through repetition rather than storage.

We need a history that does not *save* in any sense of the word; we need a history that performs. How else will we come to terms with the past of which Mendieta is a part, with a phenomenon that writers have been struggling with since the mid-1960s? How else will we be able to write ourselves out of the ill-fitting categories in which all artists of this period, not just Mendieta, are stuck? This art has emphasized performance, video, earth art, computer images, and installations—media that continually enact the cold facts of mortality and disappearance. These experiments notwithstanding, art history of this period has for the most part continued to think in terms of objects. We are willing to evaluate the disorienting effect that dematerialization has on art but not the disorienting effect that it has on our historical accounts. We retain a language that is blind to the deaths that these media encode; we say, "Isn't it beautiful how it disappears!" but, "Nonetheless, it needs to be preserved."

My interest in Ana Mendieta has been, not to present an exhaustive explanation of her life and work (if such a thing were possible), but to think as clearly as I can about her place within a set of issues that mattered in her lifetime and still matter today. I have come nowhere close to discussing all her work, and I have only hinted at some of the more rich sources of its meanings. I have tried to avoid superlative descriptions whose goal would have been to canonize this artist, to claim that she was utterly unique, that she should be added to the list of artists worthy of our attention. This is not to say that I do not think that her work is magical, dangerous, provocative, and mesmerizing. It is, rather, that I want to avoid isolating her with praise.

If Ana Mendieta's art is significant, it is because it gives evidence that postmodernity (or any other historiographic category for that matter) is not legislated from the academy but takes place in the complex lives of individuals. Mendieta's art lies at the heart of what we know to be the postmodern. It not only reflects but in fact produces the fragmentation of the subject that is one of the founding principles of that "cultural dominant." It directly engages the question of identity formation in terms of gender, sexuality, race, and class. It is also deeply indebted to the conditions of postcoloniality and the politics of the subaltern that are coterminous with the postmodern. At the same time, and very significantly, this work dramatizes the inability of that term—the *postmodern*—to cover adequately the phenomena it attempts to name. As an interpretive category, *postmodernity* is like the small box carefully padded with tissue; it is the way we try to preserve a time whose single most important characteristic is loss (the death of the author, the instability of the signifier, the victory of simulation over the real).

Inasmuch as this book is a history it is also a performance. It is empowered by the repetition of the question, "Where is Ana Mendieta?" But, as with Mendieta's branding of Eliade's book, the boundaries between history and performance are unstable. While I write my history of Ana Mendieta, she is always writing me. That is, my writing is carried out in relation to her life, a life that it can never begin to contain. Like the smoldering handprint on Eliade's book, she burns through my text unexpectedly. Mendieta and I occupy the space of history together, and, as a result, I can never achieve the privileged position *after* from which to write my history. My point here is, not to confess the abject inadequacies of the discipline of art history, but to challenge it, as Phelan puts it, "to write toward disappearance."

I wonder about Mendieta's marking, this branding of a text by fire, for it seems that the object thus produced is doubly historical, combining as it does these two different historiographic remnants, the written text and the branding. In attempting to account for the meanings produced by this work, its opposing modes of representation, its contradictory messages of claiming and annihilation, I began to read its irreconcilable tensions as an implication of my own historiographic project; it suggested to me the effects and limitations of writing a history about Ana Mendieta herself. I have learned from her that to write history is to mark the body of the other but that it is also to be marked by one's subject; it is to have one's text burned with an irrevocable and unaccountable image.

NOTES

Introduction: *Where Is Ana Mendieta?*

1 This protest was organized by the Women's Action Coalition (WAC), a women's group formed in 1991 after the Anita Hill hearings in Washington. At the time of this demonstration, the group numbered about fifteen hundred nationally and consisted largely of white women. A faction within that group was actually responsible for that part of the protest that included the banner, the T-shirts, and photocopies. This group included Raquel Mendieta, Josely Carvalho, Juan Sanchez, Mañuel Pardo, Joey Silverman, and Lucy Lippard, among others. According to Raquel Mendieta, the specific invocation of Ana Mendieta and Carl Andre by her group was not sanctioned by the larger organization because it feared alienating art world leaders loyal to or associated with Andre. For information on WAC, see Catherine S. Manegold, "No More Nice Girls," *New York Times*, 12 July 1992, pp. 25, 31. For information on the protest, see Elizabeth Hess, "Born Again," *Village Voice*, 7 July 1992, p. 38.

2 Hess, "Born Again," p. 38.

3 For a detailed account of the circumstances of Mendieta's death and the subsequent trial of Carl Andre, see Robert Katz, *Naked by the Window: The Fatal Marriage of Carl Andre and Ana Mendieta* (New York: Atlantic Monthly Press, 1990).

4   The suspicions were reignited during the trial of O. J. Simpson, who was similarly accused and later acquitted of murdering his wife. Witness the 1995 Guerrilla Girls poster featuring pictures of both men and the caption, "What do these men have in common?"

5   See Peggy Phelan, *Unmarked: The Politics of Performance* (New York: Routledge, 1993).

6   Gloria Moure, ed., *Ana Mendieta* (Barcelona: Fundació Antoni Tàpies; Santiago de Compostela: Centro Galego de Arte Contemporánea, 1997), frontispiece (emphasis added).

7   Ann Landi, "The Fifty Most Powerful People in the Art World," *Artnews*, January 1997, pp. 90–97.

8   Victor Burgin, *The End of Art Theory: Criticism and Postmodernity* (Atlantic Highlands, N.J.: Humanities Press International, 1987), 29.

9   The Museum of Modern Art's refusal in 1970 to go through with its promised distribution of an Art Workers Coalition poster depicting villagers massacred at My Lai because of a change of political heart is just one example of artists' disillusionment with the conservatism of art institutions. For more on this, see Lucy Lippard, *Get the Message? A Decade of Art for Social Change* (New York: E. P. Dutton, 1984).

10 See Victor Burgin, "The Absence of Presence: Conceptualism and Postmodernisms," in *The End of Art Theory*, 29–50.

11 Samuel Huntington, quoted in Howard Zinn, *The Twentieth Century: A People's History* (New York: Harper & Row, 1984), 259.

12 Just one example is the Civil Rights Act of 1968, which strengthened laws prohibiting violence against blacks and increased penalties for race crimes but also exempted police, the National Guard, and the military from prosecution in suppressing riots. The act was more often used against black political groups thought to be involved in instigating riots than it was to assist them. For more on this, see Harry S. Ashmore, *Civil Rights and Wrongs: A Memoir of Race and Politics, 1944–1994* (New York: Pantheon, 1994).

13 Laura Trippi and Gary Sangster, "From Trivial Pursuit to the Art of the Deal: Art Making in the Eighties," in *The Decade Show: Frameworks of Identity in the 1980s* (New York: Museum of Contemporary Hispanic Art/New Museum of Contemporary Art/Studio Museum of Harlem, 1990), 61, 63.

14 Douglas Crimp, *On the Museum's Ruins* (Cambridge, Mass.: MIT Press, 1993), 240 (Fuchs quotation), 243.

15 Joseph Roach, *Cities of the Dead: Circum-Atlantic Performance* (New York: Columbia University Press, 1996).

16 Carolee Schneemann, *More than Meat Joy*, ed. Bruce McPherson (New York: Documentext, 1979), 238–39.

17 Lucy Lippard, "Sweeping Exchanges: The Contribution of Feminism to the Art of the 1970s," *Art Journal*, Fall/Winter 1990, p. 362.

18 Abigail Solomon-Godeau, "The Legs of the Countess," *October* 39 (Winter 1986): 103.

19 Roland Barthes, "The Death of the Author," in *Image-Music-Text*, trans. Stephen Heath (New York: Hill & Wang, 1977).

20 Frank Popper, *Art Action and Participation* (New York: New York University Press, 1975), 11.

21 Bruce Nauman, quoted in Cindy Nemser, "Subject-Object Body Art," *Arts Magazine*, September–October 1971, p. 40.

22 Lucy Lippard, "The Pains and Pleasures of Rebirth: Women's Body Art," *Art in America*, May/June 1976, pp. 73–81 (reprinted as "The Pains and Pleasures of Rebirth: European and American Women's Body Art," in *From the Center: Feminist Essays on Women's Art* [New York: E. P. Dutton, 1976], 121–38).

23 Ana Mendieta, "Self Portraits" (M.A. thesis, University of Iowa, 1972).

24 Lippard, "Pains and Pleasures," 75.

25 Janet Heit, "Ana Mendieta," *Arts Magazine*, January 1980, p. 5. Jan Gura, "Ana Mendieta," in *Expressions of Self: Women and Autobiography* (New Brunswick, N.J.: Rutgers University, Douglass College Art Gallery, 1979), n.p. Christine Poggi, "The New Spiritualism," *Women Artists News*, Summer 1980, p. 6.

26 Donald Kuspit, "Ana Mendieta, Autonomous Body," in Moure, ed., *Ana Mendieta*, 50, 50, 60 n. 3. It should be noted that heterosexism lurks behind Kuspit's comments. Presumably, the reason that male artists' exclusive depictions of women are not troubling is that it is "normal" for men to be attracted to and want to represent women. Mendieta's interest in the female body is threatening in this context.

27 She had previously done another version of this performance in which guests were invited to her apartment in Iowa City, where they encountered a similarly gruesome scene.

28 Adrienne Rich, "Compulsory Heterosexuality and Lesbian Existence," *Signs* 5, no. 4 (Summer 1980): 631–60.

29 Kuspit, "Autonomous," 50.

30 Willoughby Sharp, "Notes toward an Understanding of Earth Art," in *Earth Art* (Ithaca, N.Y.: Andrew Dickson White Museum of Art, Cornell University, 1970), n.p. Thomas Leavitt, foreword to ibid., n.p. Leavitt's claim is especially interesting in the light of Rudi Fuch's 1982 comment that "we have finally built real walls" (see n. 14 above).

31 A variation of her technique of relief carving or molding includes those works in which she spread fertilizer on grass in a silhouette configuration and later photographed the grass where the resulting figure was composed of longer and greener leaves.

32 Sharp, "Notes toward an Understanding," n.p.

33 Ana Mendieta, quoted in Kittredge Cherry, "Mendieta Incorporates Herself, Earth and Art," *Daily Iowan*, 6 December 1977, p. 7.

34 In an interview, Mendieta states, "I have used gunpowder in pieces and later found that in certain rituals the *Santeros* (healers in Cuba) make 5 piles of gunpowder, light them and if they burn it means yes to the question and if they don't burn, it means no" (Linda Montano, "An Interview with Ana Mendieta," *Sulfur* 22 [Spring 1988]: 68).

35 The specific relation between these works and Mendieta's knowledge of Taino culture is taken up by Bonnie Clearwater in "The *Rupestrian Sculptures Photo Etchings*," in *Ana Mendieta: A Book of Works*, ed. Bonnie Clearwater (Miami Beach: Grassfield, 1993).

36 Gloria Feman Orenstein, "Recovering Her Story: Feminist Artists Reclaim the Great Goddess," in *The Power of Feminist Art: The American Movement of the 1970s, History and Impact*, ed. N. Broude and M. Garrard (New York: Harry N. Abrams, 1994), 177.

37 Ana Mendieta, introduction to *Dialectics of Isolation* (New York: A.I.R. Gallery, 1980), n.p.

38 See Gloria Feman Orenstein, "The Reemergence of the Archetype of the Great Goddess in Art by Contemporary Women," *Heresies* 2, no. 1 (Spring 1978): 74–84; Poggi, "The New Spiritualism," 6; and Monica Sjöö and Barbara Mor, *The Great Cosmic Mother: Rediscovering the Religion of the Earth* (San Francisco: Harper & Row, 1987).

39 For an excellent discussion of Santería's influence on Mendieta's work, see Mary Jane Jacob, in *Ana Mendieta: The "Silueta" Series, 1973–1980* (New York: Galerie Lelong, 1991).

40 Ileana Fuentes-Perez, "By Choice or by Circumstance: The Inevitable Exile of Artists," in *Fuera de Cuba/Outside Cuba: Contemporary Cuban Visual Artists/Artistas cubanos contemporaneos*, ed. Ileana Fuentes-Perez et al. (New Brunswick, N.J.: Rutgers University, Office of Hispanic Arts, Mason Gross School of the Arts, 1989), 25.

41 Philip Brenner, e.g., remarks that the Carter "administration charged that the Cuban government forced some prisoners and patients in mental institutions to emigrate at this time," making the contention seem only a politically inspired accusation (*From Confrontation to Negotiation: U.S. Relations with Cuba* [Boulder, Colo.: Westview, 1988], 23). Gillian Gunn, however, claims that "Castro forced exiles arriving to collect family members to accept common criminals and mental patients on their crafts before permitting them to leave" (*Cuba in Transition: Options for U.S. Policy* [New York: Twentieth Century Fund Press, 1993], 17).

42 Brenner, *From Confrontation to Negotiation*, 31; see also 32–33.

43 Ana's cousin Raquel Mendieta recalls in an interview that originally Castro's revolution was viewed by all Cubans as a victory over Batista's dictatorship. The perception was that "a totally tyrannical government was being rejected by the Cuban people. And the insurrectional stage of the Revolution was supported by the general population, by all social classes. At that time the

family was unanimously a Revolutionary family" (Nereyda Garcia-Ferraz, "An Interview with Raquel [Kaki] Mendieta," Sulfur 22 [Spring 1988]: 62).

44 Fuentes-Perez, "By Choice or by Circumstance," 21–22.

45 Luis Camnitzer, New Art of Cuba (Austin: University of Texas Press, 1994), 93.

46 Ibid., 91–92.

47 Henry Sayre, The Object of Performance: The American Avant-Garde since 1970 (Chicago: University of Chicago Press, 1989).

48 See Judith Butler, Gender Trouble: Feminism and the Subversion of Identity (New York: Routledge, 1990), and Bodies That Matter: On the Discursive Limits of Sex (New York: Routledge, 1993); and Phelan, Unmarked.

49 See Jacques Derrida, "Signature, Event, Context," Glyph 1–2 (1977): 172–97; and J. L. Austin, How to Do Things with Words, ed. J. O. Urmson and Marina Sbisà (Cambridge, Mass.: Harvard University Press, 1975).

50 Butler, Gender Trouble, 16.

51 Phelan, Unmarked, 3.

52 Butler gives a feminist interpretation of Austin by considering how performatives like "It's a girl!" interpellate gender through what she calls "girling" (Bodies That Matter, 7). Compare this with Austin's less critical How to Do Things with Words.

53 Derrida, "Signature, Event, Context," 186.

54 Edward Said, "The Mind of Winter: Reflections on Exile," Harper's, September 1984, p. 50.

Chapter 1 Fire

1 Mendieta had this branding iron fabricated at the sculpture foundry at the University of Iowa in the early 1970s. She used it in a variety of other works to brand earth or grass, but in only one other work did she brand a book. This was a blank artist's sketchbook, which she branded in 1978.

2 Diana Fuss, Essentially Speaking: Feminism, Nature and Difference (New York: Routledge, 1989); Naomi Schor and Elizabeth Weed, eds., The Essential Difference (Bloomington: Indiana University Press, 1994).

3 Butler, Gender Trouble, 16.

4 Naomi Schor, introduction to Schor and Weed, eds., The Essential Difference, xii.

5 Butler, Bodies That Matter, 227–28.

6 Trinh T. Minh-ha, Woman, Native, Other (Bloomington: Indiana University Press, 1989), 48.

7 Butler, Bodies That Matter, 8.

8 Jacques Derrida, Cinders, trans. and ed. Ned Lukacher (Lincoln: University of Nebraska Press, 1991), 49, 53.

9 Rebecca Schneider, The Explicit Body in Performance (London: Routledge, 1997), 119.

10 Miwon Kwon, "Bloody Valentines: Afterimages by Ana Mendieta," in Inside

the Visible: An Elliptical Traverse of 20th Century Art in, of, and from the Feminine, ed. Catherine M. de Zegher (Cambridge, Mass.: MIT Press, 1996), 167, 168.

11 Ana Mendieta, "Ana Mendieta: A Selection of Statements and Notes," Sulfur 22 (Spring 1988): 72. In addition, the statement is quoted in Katz, Naked by the Window, 123. It also appears in Cuba/USA: The First Generation (Washington, D.C.: Fondo del Sol Visual Arts Center, 1991), 56; and it is read in the video Ana Mendieta: Fuego de Tierra, dir. Kate Horsfield, Nereyda Garcia-Ferraz, and Branda Miller (1987), distributed by Women Make Movies, New York.

12 Octavio Paz, The Labyrinth of Solitude: Life and Thought in Mexico, trans. Lysander Kemp (New York: Grove, 1961), 85.

13 Butler, Bodies That Matter, 224.

14 Mircea Eliade, The Myth of the Eternal Return; or, Cosmos and History (1954), trans. Willard R. Trask (Princeton, N.J.: Princeton University Press, 1965), xv (for the recommendation), xviii.

15 Ana Mendieta, in Intermedia, ed. Hans Breder and Stephen C. Foster (Iowa City: Corroboree Gallery of New Concepts, School of Art and Art History, University of Iowa, 1980), 119.

16 Mircea Eliade, Rites and Symbols of Initiation (New York: Harper & Row, 1958), xii.

17 Eliade, Cosmos and History, 20.

18 Eliade, Rites and Symbols, xiii.

19 Ibid., 51.

20 Ibid., 6, 26. Many of Mendieta's works involve the ritual use of blood, which she considered to be a powerful symbolic and spiritual substance, a fluid through which flow the "original beliefs" (see Mendieta, "A Selection of Statements and Notes," 72; and Jacob, in Ana Mendieta, 10–12).

21 Eliade, Rites and Symbols, 85.

22 Ana Mendieta, in Clearwater, ed., Ana Mendieta, 22–23.

23 Eliade, Cosmos and History, 155, 87, 155–56.

24 Ibid., 157, 156.

25 Eliade, Rites and Symbols, ix, and Cosmos and History, 149.

26 Eliade, Cosmos and History, xii.

27 Ibid., xi.

28 Fuss, Essentially Speaking, 4.

29 Eliade, Cosmos and History, 111.

30 Phelan, Unmarked, 6.

Chapter 2   Earth

1 Alan Sonfist, introduction to Art in the Land: A Critical Anthology of Environmental Art, ed. Alan Sonfist (New York: E. P. Dutton, 1983), xi–xii.

2 Mira Schor, Wet: On Painting, Feminism, and Art Culture (Durham, N.C.: Duke University Press, 1997), 63, 66 (quotation).

3 Kwon, "Bloody Valentines," 167.

4 Records of the A.I.R. Gallery.

5 B. Ruby Rich, "The Screaming Silence," *Village Voice*, 16–23 September 1996, p. 24.

6 Butler, *Bodies That Matter*, 225.

7 Homi Bhabha, "DissemiNation: Time, Narrative, and the Margins of the Modern Nation," in *Nation and Narration*, ed. Homi Bhabha (New York: Routledge, 1990), 294 (quotation), 297.

8 After Fidel Castro came to power in 1959, the U.S. government, under both Presidents Eisenhower and Kennedy, took an increasingly confrontational stance in its dealings with Cuba. In January 1961, Eisenhower broke diplomatic ties to the island in response to its increasingly socialistic structure, its strengthening ties to Czechoslovakia, and the nationalization of its oil refineries. For more on the history of U.S.-Cuban relations, see Brenner, *From Confrontation to Negotiation*, 13; Wayne Smith, *The Closest of Enemies: A Personal and Diplomatic Account of U.S.-Cuban Relations since 1957* (New York: W. W. Norton, 1987); and Gunn, *Cuba in Transition*.

9 Katz, *Naked by the Window*, 38.

10 In an interview with the author, 10 August 1994, Raquel Mendieta explained that her family had had a long and illustrious history in Cuba. Her father's role in the revolution is spelled out more fully in Katz, *Naked by the Window*, 40.

11 Katz, *Naked by the Window*, 42, 135.

12 Félix Roberto Masud-Piloto, *With Open Arms: Cuban Migration to the United States* (Totowa, N.J.: Rowan & Littlefield, 1988), 39.

13 Fuentes-Perez, "By Choice or by Circumstance," 21 (both quotations).

14 Raquel (Kaki) Mendieta, quoted in Garcia-Ferraz, "An Interview with Raquel (Kaki) Mendieta," 62. In this interview, Raquel goes on to say that religion played a central role in Ana's parents' decision. She claims that the Catholic church had begun the *patria potestad* or "paternal authority" campaign, which "would allege that the Revolution and communism wanted to take children away from their parents, to take away their authority, the rights parents have regarding the education of their children."

15 Bryan O. Walsh, "Cuban Refugee Children," *Journal of Inter-American Studies and World Affairs* 13, nos. 3–4 (July–October 1971): 402, 390–91.

16 Once in the United States, the children's care was overseen by the Cuban Children's Program, an organization funded by the U.S. State Department and coordinated by various religious and civic groups. For a more detailed account of Operation Pedro Pan and the Cuban Children's Program, see Masud-Piloto, *With Open Arms*, 39–43; and Carlos Cortés, ed., *Cuban Refugee Programs* (New York: Arno, 1980).

17 Raquel Mendieta, interview with the author, 10 August 1994.

18 Mañuel Pardo, interview with the author, 14 May 1996.

19 Raquel (Kaki) Mendieta Costa, "Silhouette," trans. David Frye, *Michigan Quarterly Review* 33, no. 3 (Summer 1994): 551.

20 Raquel painfully recalls an incident in which her snow boots were returned to the store when it was discovered that their purchase exceeded the monthly stipend from Catholic Charities. She spent part of an Iowa winter without boots because it was determined that what belonged to her could not exceed the limits of that charity. Raquel Mendieta, interview with the author, 10 August 1994.

21 Quoted in Mendieta Costa, "Silhouette," 552.

22 Ana Mendieta, introduction to *Dialectics of Isolation,* n.p.

23 Eduardo Costa, untitled essay in *Sulfur* 22 (Spring 1988): 82. Costa writes, "Although critical of our economic system she believed in America's spirit as a force that would survive Capitalism." Both here and in the catalog *Cuba/USA: The First Generation,* Costa downplays Mendieta's pro-Castro politics. In Mendieta's obituary in the feminist art journal *Heresies,* the editors describe her more strongly as having become "a passionate supporter of the Revolution" ("Ana Mendieta, 1948–1985," *Heresies* 5, no. 2 [1985]: n.p.).

24 Ana Mendieta, introduction to *Dialectics of Isolation,* n.p.

25 Trinh, *Woman, Native, Other,* 98.

26 Montano, "An Interview with Ana Mendieta," 66.

27 Ana Mendieta, in Breder and Foster, eds., *Intermedia,* 119.

28 Sherry B. Ortner, "Is Female to Male as Nature Is to Culture?" *Feminist Studies* 1, no. 2 (Fall 1972): 11.

29 Eliade, *Cosmos and History,* 157.

30 Mendieta, "A Collection of Statements and Notes," 71.

31 Tuula Karjalainen, "The Mark of a Woman," in *Ana Mendieta, 1948–1985* (Helsinki: Helsinki City Art Museum, 1996), 16.

32 Mary Sabbatino, "Ana Mendieta *Silueta* Works: Sources and Influences," in *Ana Mendieta* (Helsinki City Art Museum), 48.

33 Charles Merewether, "Displacement and the Reinvention of Identity," in *Latin American Artists of the Twentieth Century,* ed. Waldo Rasmussen (New York: Museum of Modern Art, 1993), 146.

34 Caren Kaplan, "Deterritorializations: The Rewriting of Home and Exile in Western Feminist Discourse," *Cultural Critique* 6 (Spring 1987): 188.

35 Paz, *Labyrinth,* 20.

36 Mary Beth Edelson, *Seven Cycles: Public Rituals* (n.p., 1980), 17.

37 See Carol Christ and Judith Plaskow, eds., *Womanspirit Rising: A Feminist Reader in Religion* (San Francisco: Harper & Row, 1979); and Christine Downing, *The Goddess: Mythological Images of the Feminine* (New York: Crossroad, 1981).

38 Mendieta, "A Selection of Statements and Notes," 71.

39 Mendieta, introduction to *Dialectics of Isolation,* n.p.

40 Paz, *Labyrinth,* 14–15. It is interesting to note that Mendieta seems to have missed the negative terms in which Paz interpreted the pachuco (see Marcos

Sanchez-Tranquilino and John Tagg, "The Pachuco's Flayed Hide: The Museum, Identity, and Buenas Garras," in *Chicano Art: Resistance and Affirmation, 1965–1985*, ed. Richard Griswold del Castillo et al. [Los Angeles: Wight Art Gallery, University of California, 1991], 99–100).

41 Sanchez-Tranquilino and Tagg, "The Pachuco's Flayed Hide," 102.

42 Katz, *Naked by the Window*, 282.

43 Bhabha, "DissemiNation," 300, 312.

44 Lucy Lippard, *Overlay* (New York: Pantheon, 1983), 49.

45 Ana Mendieta, quoted in Montano, "An Interview with Ana Mendieta," 67.

46 Austin, *How to Do Things with Words*, 4–7.

47 Schor, *Wet*, 63.

Chapter 3   Exile

1 Sigmund Freud, "The 'Uncanny,'" in *The Standard Edition of the Complete Psychological Works of Sigmund Freud*, ed. and trans. James Strachey (London: Hogarth, 1955), 17:224.

2 Ibid., 241.

3 Ibid., 223, 225.

4 Freud demonstrates this meaning of the unheimlich through a discussion of E. T. A. Hoffmann's story "The Sand Man" (ibid., 227–33). For Freud, such memories can also be tied to castration fears (pp. 231–33), a connection that, although intriguing, is ancillary to the present discussion and well beyond the scope of this text.

5 Ibid., 234, 237, 235, 224–25.

6 Montano, "An Interview with Ana Mendieta," 67.

7 Freud, "The 'Uncanny,'" 236.

8 I owe this phrase to Della Pollock.

9 Charles Merewether, "From Inscription to Dissolution: An Essay on Expenditure in the Work of Ana Mendieta," in Moure, ed., *Ana Mendieta*, 110.

10 Timothy Brennan, "The National Longing for Form," in Bhabha, ed., *Nation and Narration*, 47, 50.

11 Benedict Anderson, *Imagined Communities: Reflections on the Origin and Spread of Nationalism* (London: Verso, 1983), 6.

12 Freud, "The 'Uncanny,'" 226.

13 Bhabha, "DissemiNation," 295.

14 Julia Kristeva, *Strangers to Ourselves*, trans. Leon S. Roudiez (New York: Columbia University Press, 1991), 187.

15 "Ana Mendieta, 1948–1985" (*Heresies*). Poggi, "The New Spiritualism," 6. John Perreault, "Ana Mendieta (1948–1985)," *Sulfur* 22 (Spring 1988): 56.

16 Coco Fusco, "Displacement: Traces of Ana Mendieta," *Poliester* 4 (1992): 52 (emphasis added).

17 Ana Mendieta, quoted in Judith Wilson, "Ana Mendieta Plants Her Garden," *Village Voice*, 13–19 August 1980, p. 71.

18 John Perreault, "Earth and Fire: Mendieta's Body of Work," in *Ana Mendieta: A Retrospective* (New York: New Museum of Contemporary Art, 1987), 13.

19 Ana Mendieta, quoted in Raquel Mendieta, "Ana Mendieta: Self-Portrait of a Goddess," *Review: Latin American Literature and Arts* 39 (January–June 1988): 39, quoted in Nancy Spero, "Tracing Ana Mendieta," *Artforum*, April 1992, p. 76.

20 Freud, "The 'Uncanny,'" 226.

21 Gloria Anzaldúa, *Borderlands/La frontera: The New Mestiza* (San Francisco: Aunt Lute, 1987), 3.

22 In addition to the themes of nation and earth that make this work of interest to me, it is also clearly related to the theme of resurrection. It, along with another work that she executed a year earlier in Iowa, was influenced by an article that she read in *National Geographic* on Easter rituals in the Greek Orthodox church. In the earlier piece, she constructed a small raft using red velvet cloth stretched over a frame made of sticks. She made a figure out of flower petals similar to the one she made in this work and then filmed the raft as it floated down the Iowa River. The article includes a photograph showing rose petals used to symbolize the body of Christ (see Howard La Fay, "Where Jesus Walked," *National Geographic* 132, no. 6 [1967]: 775).

23 Raquel Mendieta, interview with the author, 10 August 1994.

24 Mendieta, "A Selection of Statements and Notes," 71.

25 Kristeva, *Strangers to Ourselves*, 5.

26 Perreault, "Earth and Fire," 13.

27 Freud, "The 'Uncanny,'" 245.

28 Said, "The Mind of Winter," 53.

29 Ibid., 49, 50.

30 Ibid., 51.

31 The practice of dirt eating, or geophagy, was once widespread in the Southern United States. It has been traced to cultures around the world, but the practice was brought to the United States by West African slaves. It seems to serve a variety of purposes: as a dietary mineral supplement for pregnant women, as a means to stave off hunger during periods of famine, as a medicine, and, as in the story of the brides, as a means of acculturation (see John M. Hunter, "Geophagy in Africa and in the United States: A Culture-Nutrition Hypothesis," *Geographical Review* 63, no. 2 [April 1973]: 170–95).

32 James Clifford, "On Ethnographic Allegory," in *Writing Culture: The Poetics and Politics of Ethnography*, ed. James Clifford and George E. Marcus (Berkeley and Los Angeles: University of California Press, 1986), 98.

33 Ibid., 116, 109.

34 Henri Junod, *The Life of a South African Tribe* (1912; reprint, New Hyde Park,

N.Y.: University Books, 1962), 49 n. 1. It is important to note that, although Junod's native language was French, he actually wrote this text in English.

35 Lucien Lévy-Bruhl, *The Primitive Mentality*, trans. Lilian A. Clare (New York: Macmillan, 1923), 214. It is worthwhile noting that the original French title of Lévy-Bruhl's book is *Les fonctions mentales dans les sociétés inférieures*.

36 Ana Mendieta, quoted in Petra Barreras del Rio, "Ana Mendieta: A Historical Overview," in *Ana Mendieta: A Retrospective*, 31.

37 Gylbert Coker, "Ana Mendieta at A.I.R.," *Art in America*, April 1980, p. 134.

38 Junod, *The Life of a South African Tribe*, 7, iv, 9.

39 Ibid., 49 (quotation), 48, 49.

40 Mendieta, "A Selection of Statements and Notes," 72.

41 Lévy-Bruhl, *The Primitive Mentality*, 214.

42 Ibid., 215.

43 Arnold van Gennep, *The Rites of Passage* (Chicago: University of Chicago Press, 1960), 11.

44 Victor Turner, *From Ritual to Theatre: The Human Seriousness of Play* (New York: PAJ, 1982), 44–45.

45 Mendieta, "A Selection of Statements and Notes," 72.

46 Although Junod does not use the word *nation*, neither does he use *village* or *region*. Rather, he explains that the story is a "case of moving from one country to another" (*The Life of a South African Tribe*, 49).

47 Keith Irvine, foreword to Junod, *The Life of a South African Tribe*, viii.

48 Junod, *The Life of a South African Tribe*, 11.

49 According to Raquel Mendieta (see Garcia-Ferraz, "An Interview with Raquel [Kaki] Mendieta," 65).

Chapter 4   Travel

1 Mendieta, "A Selection of Statements and Notes," 70, 71.

2 Coker, "Ana Mendieta at A.I.R.," 134. Poggi, "The New Spiritualism," 6. Spero, "Tracing Ana Mendieta," 77. Charles Merewether writes that Mendieta's works were an "attempt to overcome the experience of displacement" ("Displacement and the Reinvention of Identity," 146); Tuula Karjalainen discusses Mendieta's "traumatic separation from home and country" (*Ana Mendieta, 1948–1985*, 16); and Heidi Rauch and Federico Suro claim that "Mendieta used her art to heal herself" (Heidi Rauch and Federico Suro, "Ana Mendieta's Primal Scream," *Américas* 44, no. 5 [1992]: 48).

3 Perreault, "Earth and Fire," 14.

4 Georges Van Den Abbeele, *Travel as Metaphor: From Montaigne to Rousseau* (Minneapolis: University of Minnesota Press, 1992), xvii–xviii.

5 Anderson, *Imagined Communities*, 115.

6 The literature on drag and cross-dressing is wide-ranging. See, e.g., Eve

Sedgwick and Michael Moon, "Divinity: A Dossier, a Performance Piece, a Little-Understood Emotion," in *Tendencies*, by Eve Kosofsky Sedgwick (Durham, N.C.: Duke University Press, 1993): "In the film and theater of the past two decades, as well as in the body of critical gender theory and performance theory that has arisen during the same period, transvestism has often been trivialized and domesticated into mere 'crossdressing,' as if its practice had principally to do with something that can be put on and off as easily as a costume" (p. 219). Here, Sedgwick and Moon are responding to Elaine Showalter, "Critical Cross-Dressing: Male Feminists and the Woman of the Year," in *Men in Feminism*, ed. Alice Jardine and Paul Smith (New York: Methuen, 1987). In another vein, Peggy Phelan sees drag as part of a regulatory economy of gender when she writes, "Perhaps the best performative example of the phallic function is the theatre of drag. A man imitates an image of woman in order to confirm that she belongs to him. . . . Performing the image of what he is not allows him to dramatize himself as 'all' " (*Unmarked*, 17). See also Butler, *Gender Trouble* (esp. chap. 3, "Subversive Bodily Acts"), and the introduction and chaps. 4 and 6 of *Bodies That Matter*; and Marjorie Garber, *Vested Interests: Cross Dressing and Cultural Anxiety* (New York: Routledge, 1992).

7   Pliny the Elder, *The Elder Pliny's Chapters on the History of Art*, Book XXV, trans. K. Jex-Blake (Chicago: Argonaut, 1968), 175.

8   Freud, "The 'Uncanny,' " 235.

9   Ana Mendieta, quoted in Wilson, "Ana Mendieta Plants Her Garden," 71.

10 Bhabha, "DissemiNation," 300.

11 Gerardo Mosquera, "Esculturas Rupestres de Ana Mendieta," *Arieto* 7, no. 28 (1981): 54: "Habitadas antaño por los indios, fueron después refugio de cimarrones y de luchadores de las guerras de independencia. En la gruta de Sitio Perdido funcionó un hospital de sangre durante la contienda de 1895, y en ella murió un general del Ejército Libertador. A lo largo de la historia pasada de Cuba las Escaleras fueron un abrigo natural para rebeldes y perseguidos."

12 Quoted in Katz, *Naked by the Window*, 144.

13 Quoted in Fusco, "Displacement," 61.

14 Hans Breder, quoted in Katz, *Naked by the Window*, 144.

15 Anzaldúa, *Borderlands/La frontera*, 3.

16 I owe this phrase to Della Pollock.

17 Fusco, "Displacement," 61.

18 Turner, *From Ritual to Theatre*, 27.

19 Anzaldúa, *Borderlands/La frontera*, 20.

20 Raquel Mendieta, interview with the author, 10 August 1994.

21 Katz, *Naked by the Window*, 315.

22 Raquel Mendieta, interview with the author, 10 August 1994.

23 Hans Breder, "Ana Mendieta: Imprints/Student Years, 1972–77," *Sulfur* 22 (Spring 1988): 74–75.

24 Sharp, "Notes toward an Understanding," n.p.

25 Roland Barthes, *Camera Lucida: Reflections on Photography*, trans. Richard Howard (New York: Hill & Wang, 1981), 96.

26 Ibid., 12.

27 Phelan, *Unmarked*, 27.

28 See chap. 1, n. 11, above.

29 Anzaldúa, *Borderlands/La frontera*, 3.

30 A story aired on National Public Radio's "Weekend Edition" on 5 February 1994 that described a relevant situation in Naco, Arizona, a small border town. After enduring a series of robberies, believed to have been committed by Mexicans who slipped back across the border to elude capture, the town decided to build a steel wall along the border. Some citizens pointed out that the planned wall might evoke associations with the Berlin Wall and cautioned that this was not an image that the town wanted to produce. It was decided instead that the town would build a white picket fence twelve feet high along the border. The NPR story was framed by references to Robert Frost's famous maxim, "Good fences make good neighbors."

31 Guillermo Gomez-Peña, "Border Culture: The Multicultural Paradigm," in *The Decade Show*, 93.

32 Juan Flores and George Yudice, "Living Borders/Buscando America: Languages of Latino Self-Formation," *Social Text* 24 (1990): 59.

33 Gomez-Peña, "Border Culture," 96.

Chapter 5   Body

1 Fuss, *Essentially Speaking*, 32.

2 Ana Mendieta, "La Venus Negra, Based on a Cuban Legend," *Heresies* 4, no. 1 (1981): 22. I suspect that Mendieta has taken this almost verbatim from Samuel Feijóo, *Mitos y leyendas en las villas* (Havana: Universidad Central de las Villas, 1965), 61–64. Feijóo must in turn have taken it from Adrian del Valle, *Tradiciones y leyendas de Cienfuegos* (Havana: Sociedad Editorial Cuba Contemporánea, 1919), 117–24.

3 Before they knew what was happening, the Spaniards had so totally annihilated the Siboney that an archaeological investigation of their culture in 1941 would turn up only a few shells and bones (see Cornelius Osgood, "The Ciboney Culture of Cayo Redondo, Cuba," *Yale University Publications in Anthropology*, nos. 25–26 [1942]: 5–71).

4 See Jaime Suchlicki, *Cuba from Columbus to Castro* (Washington, D.C.: Brassey's, 1990), 53–58.

5 Robert L. Paquette, *Sugar Is Made with Blood: The Conspiracy of La Escalera in the Conflict between Empires over Slavery in Cuba* (Middletown, Conn.: Wesleyan University Press, 1988), 258. Here, Paquette refers to the Cuban literary movement known as *siboneyisme*, whose leader was Gabriel de la Concepción Valdés,

known as Plácido. Paquette writes that this movement "took hold among Plácido's young, educated white countrymen and . . . served by its selection and romanticization of Indian themes to attack Spanish rule and to inspire anticolonial thinking and indigenous nationalism" (p. 258).

6 Suchlicki, *Cuba from Columbus to Castro,* 57.

7 Butler, *Gender Trouble,* viii.

8 I do not want to overstate the possibility for the empowerment of these subaltern groups. The threat posed by performing the liminality of race and gender is, as I noted in chap. 3, what Victor Turner calls a "subversive flicker." He writes that "it is put into the service of normativeness almost as soon as it appears. Yet I see it as a kind of institutional capsule or pocket which contains the germ of future social developments" (*From Ritual to Theatre,* 44–45).

9 For more on the sexual implications of the black female body and the ambivalent feelings about it, see Sander Gilman, "The Hottentot and the Prostitute: Toward an Iconography of Female Sexuality," in *Difference and Pathology: Stereotypes of Sexuality, Race, and Madness* (Ithaca, N.Y.: Cornell University Press, 1985).

10 Tzvetan Todorov, *The Conquest of America: The Question of the Other,* trans. Richard Howard (New York: Harper & Row, 1984), 48–49. See also Bartolomé de las Casas, *Brevissima relacion de la destruycion de los Indios* (Seville, 1552).

11 Eduardo Galeano, *Open Veins of Latin America: Five Centuries of the Pillage of a Continent,* trans. Cedric Belfrage (New York: Monthly Review Press, 1973), 79–83, 75 ("monocultures"), 80.

12 Butler, *Gender Trouble,* 24.

13 Butler confirms this possibility in her discussion of passing in "Passing, Queering: Nella Larsen's Psychoanalytic Challenge," in *Bodies That Matter,* 167–85.

14 Richard Dyer, "White," *Screen* 29, no. 24 (Autumn 1988): 46.

15 Todorov, *The Conquest of America,* 21.

16 Galeano, *Open Veins of Latin America,* 206. Galeano is quoting from Mario Margulis, *Migración y marginalidad en la sociedad argentina* (Buenos Aires, 1968).

17 Suchlicki, *Cuba from Columbus to Castro,* 30. Accurate figures to demonstrate this are hard to find since it was in Cuba's interest to hide the numbers of Africans being brought to the island after slavery was abolished in 1879. According to Verena Martinez-Alier, in 1846 there were 472,985 blacks and mulattoes and 425,767 whites (*Marriage, Class and Colour in Nineteenth Century Cuba: A Study of Racial Attitudes and Sexual Values in a Slave Society* [Cambridge: Cambridge University Press, 1974], 3).

18 Paquette, *Sugar Is Made with Blood,* 92, 87 (quotation).

19 Ana Mendieta quoted in *112 Workshop/112 Greene Street: History Artists and Artworks,* ed. Robyn Brentano and Mark Savitt (New York: New York University Press, 1981), 278.

20 Michelle Rosaldo, "The Use and Abuse of Anthropology: Reflections on

Feminism and Cross-Cultural Understanding," *Signs* 5, no. 3 (Spring 1980): 392.

21 The United States has long used the rule of "hypodescent" to distinguish among races. This rule suggests that blackness is defined by blood, that one drop of black blood makes a person black. Thus, the distinction is seemingly made clear: there are only two colors, white and black, and they have little or nothing to do with appearance. This kind of distinction facilitates segregation: if there is not a spectrum of colors with which to contend but only two, segregation is a simple matter. F. James Davis explains that, although most states in the United States no longer define race according to the "one-drop rule," it is still used as a commonly accepted definition, one that informs governmental and judicial pronouncements on race. He cites the 1985 case (which was finally appealed to the Supreme Court in 1986) in which a woman, classified on her birth certificate as black according to the "one-drop rule," attempted unsuccessfully to change her race to white (*Who Is Black: One Nation's Definition* [University Park, Pa.: Pennsylvania State University Press, 1991], 8–11). For more on this, see Carlos Moore, "Congo or Carabalí? Race Relations in Socialist Cuba," *Caribbean Review* 15, no. 2 (Spring 1986): 12–15, 43; Charles Wagley, "On the Concept of Social Race in the Americas," in *Contemporary Cultures and Societies of Latin America: A Reader in the Social Anthropology of Middle and South America and the Caribbean*, ed. Dwight B. Heath and Richard N. Abrams (New York: Random House, 1965), 531–44; and David Booth, "Cuba, Color and the Revolution," *Science and Society* 40, no. 2 (Summer 1976): 129–72.

22 Ana Mendieta, introduction to *Dialectics of Isolation*, n.p.

23 Roberto Fernández Retamar, *Caliban and Other Essays*, trans. Edward Baker (Minneapolis: University of Minnesota Press, 1989), 16.

24 José Martí, *En Los Estados Unidos* (Madrid: El Libro de Bolsillo Alianza Editorial, 1968), 304. It is important to keep in mind that, when Martí uses the word *America*, he is referring to the Americas and specifically what is called *Latin America* in the United States. However, since *America* is so often read as synonymous with *the United States*, I have chosen to use the designation *Latin America* to avoid confusion.

25 Joan Griscom, "On Healing the Nature/History Split in Feminist Thought," *Heresies* 4, no. 1 (1981): 7.

26 Bhabha, "Introduction: Narrating the Nation," in Bhabha, ed., *Nation and Narration*, 4.

Conclusion: Writing toward Disappearance

1 Phelan, *Unmarked*, 7.

BIBLIOGRAPHY

A.I.R. Gallery. *Dialectics of Isolation: An Exhibition of Third World Women Artists of the U.S.* New York, 1980.

———. *Rupestrian Sculptures/Esculturas Rupestres*. New York, 1981.

Amos, Valerie, and Pratibha Parmar. "Challenging Imperial Feminism." *Feminist Review* 17 (Autumn 1984): 3–20.

"Ana Mendieta, 1948–1985." *Heresies* 5, no. 2 (1985): n.p.

Anderson, Benedict. *Imagined Communities: Reflections on the Origin and Spread of Nationalism*. London: Verso, 1983.

Anzaldúa, Gloria. *Borderlands/La frontera: The New Mestiza*. San Francisco: Spinsters/Aunt Lute, 1987.

———, ed. *Making Face, Making Soul/Haciendo caras: Creative and Critical Perspectives by Feminists of Color*. San Francisco: Aunt Lute, 1990.

Arron, José Juan. *Leyendas cubanas*. Havana: Editorial Arte y Literatura, 1978.

Beardsley, John. *Earthworks and Beyond: Contemporary Art in the Landscape*. New York: Abbeville, 1984.

Bhabha, Homi K., ed. *Nation and Narration*. New York: Routledge, 1990.

Bolivar, Simon. *Selected Writings of Bolivar*. Edited by Harold A. Bierck Jr. Translated by Lewis Bertrand. New York: Colonial, 1951.

Booth, David. "Cuba, Color, and the Revolution." *Science and Society* 40, no. 2 (Summer 1976): 1–33.

Borras, Maria Lluisa, and Antonio Zaya. *Cuba siglo XX: Modernidad y sincretismo*. Las Palmas de Gran Canaria: Centro Atlantico de Arte Moderno; Palma: Fundacío la Caixo; Barcelona: Centre d'Art Santa Monica, 1996.

Breder, Hans, and Stephen C. Foster. *Intermedia*. Iowa City: Corroboree, Gallery of New Concepts, University of Iowa, 1980.

Brenner, Philip. *From Confrontation to Negotiation: U.S. Relations with Cuba*. Boulder, Colo.: Westview, 1988.

Brentano, Robyn, and Mark Savitt. *112 Workshop/112 Greene Street: History, Artists and Artwork*. New York: New York University Press, 1981.

Broude, Norma, and Mary D. Garrard, eds. *The Power of Feminist Art: The American Movement of the 1970s, History and Impact*. New York: Harry N. Abrams, 1994.

Butler, Judith. *Gender Trouble: Feminism and the Subversion of Identity*. New York: Routledge, 1990.

————. *Bodies That Matter: On the Discursive Limits of Sex*. New York: Routledge, 1993.

Cabrera, Lydia. *El monte*. Miami: Rema, 1968.

————. *Cuentos negros de Cuba*. Madrid: Ramos, 1972.

Camnitzer, Luis. *New Art of Cuba*. Austin: University of Texas Press, 1994.

Chadwick, Whitney. *Woman, Art, and Society*. New York: Thames & Hudson, 1990.

Cherry, Kitteredge. "Mendieta Incorporates Herself, Earth and Art." *Daily Iowan*, 6 December 1977, p. 7.

Chomski, Noam. *Year 501: The Conquest Continues*. Boston: South End, 1993.

Clearwater, Bonnie, ed. *Ana Mendieta: A Book of Works*. Miami Beach: Grassfield, 1993.

Clifford, James. "On Ethnographic Allegory." In *Writing Culture: The Poetics and Politics of Ethnography*, ed. James Clifford and George Marcus. Berkeley and Los Angeles: University of California Press, 1986.

Coker, Gylbert. "Ana Mendieta at A.I.R." *Art in America*, April 1980, pp. 133–34.

Coon, Carleton. *The Living Races of Man*. New York: Alfred A. Knopf, 1969.

Cortés, Carlos E., ed. *Cuban Refugee Programs*. New York: Arno, 1980.

Daly, Mary. *Beyond God the Father: Toward a Philosophy of Women's Liberation*. Boston: Beacon, 1973.

Davis, F. James. *Who Is Black: One Nation's Definition*. University Park, Pa.: Pennsylvania State University Press, 1991.

Derrida, Jacques. "Signature, Event, Context." *Glyph* 1–2 (1977): 172–97.

————. *Limited, Inc*. Evanston, Ill.: Northwestern University Press, 1988.

Douglass College Art Gallery. *Expressions of Self: Women and Autobiography*. New Brunswick, N.J.: Douglass College Art Gallery, Rutgers University, 1979.

Dryer, Richard. "White." *Screen* 29, no. 4 (Autumn 1988): 44–64.

Eliade, Mircea. *The Myth of the Eternal Return; or, Cosmos and History*. 1954. Translated by Willard R. Trask. Princeton, N.J.: Princeton University Press, 1965.

————. *Rites and Symbols of Initiation: The Mysteries of Birth and Rebirth*. Translated by Willard R. Trask. New York: Harper & Row, 1958.

Eshleman, Clayton, and Caryl Eshleman, eds. "Earth from Cuba, Sand from Vara-
dero: A Tribute to Ana Mendieta." *Sulfur* (Eastern Michigan University) 22
(Spring 1988): 54–114.

Feijóo, Samuel. *Mitos y leyendas en las villas.* Havana: Universidad Central de las
Villas, 1965.

———. *Mitologia cubana.* Havana: Editorial Letras Cubanas, 1986.

Fisher Gallery. *Aquí: 27 Latin American Artists Living and Working in the United States.* Los
Angeles: Fisher Gallery, University of Southern California, 1984.

Flores, Juan, and George Yudice. "Living Borders/Buscando America: Languages
of Self-Formation." *Social Text* 24 (1990): 51–84.

Fondo del Sol Visual Arts Center. *Cuba-USA: The First Generation.* Washington, D.C.:
Fondo del Sol Visual Arts Center, 1991.

Freud, Sigmund. "The Uncanny." In *The Standard Edition of the Complete Psychological Works of Sigmund Freud,* ed. and trans. James Strachey, vol. 17. London:
Hogarth, 1955.

Fuentes-Perez, Ileana, et al., eds. *Fuera de Cuba: Contemporary Cuban Visual Artists/Artis-
tas cubanos contemporaneos.* New Brunswick, N.J.: Rutgers University, Office of
Hispanic Arts, Mason Gross School of the Arts, 1989.

Fusco, Coco. "Displacement: Traces of Ana Mendieta." *Poliester* 4 (1992): 52–61.

Fuss, Diana. *Essentially Speaking: Feminism, Nature and Difference.* New York: Routledge, 1989.

Gadon, Elinor W. *The Once and Future Goddess: A Symbol for Our Time.* New York: Harper
& Row, 1988.

Galeano, Eduardo. *Open Veins of Latin America: Five Centuries of the Pillage of a Continent.*
New York: Monthly Review Press, 1973.

Gilman, Sander L. "The Hottentot and the Prostitute." In *Difference and Pathology:
Stereotypes of Sexuality, Race, and Madness.* Ithaca, N.Y.: Cornell University Press,
1985.

Greenville County Museum of Art. *Just Like a Woman.* Greenville, S.C.: Emrys Foun-
dation/Greenville County Museum of Art, 1988.

Griswold del Castillo, Richard, Teresa McKenna, and Yvonne Yarbro-Bejarano,
eds. *Chicano Art: Resistance and Affirmation, 1965–1985.* Los Angeles: Wight Art
Gallery, University of California, 1990.

Hammond, Harmony. *Wrappings.* New York: ISL Mussman Bruce, 1984.

Harris, Nancy Lynn. "The Female Imagery of Mary Beth Edelson and Ana Mendieta." M.F.A. thesis, Louisiana State University, 1978.

Heit, Janet. "Ana Mendieta." *Arts Magazine,* January 1980, p. 5.

———. "Seeking the Measure of Feminist Art." *Women Artists News,* April 1980, p. 3.

Helms, Mary W. *Ulysses' Sail: An Ethnographic Odyssey of Power, Knowledge, and Geographic
Distance.* Princeton, N.J.: Princeton University Press, 1988.

Helsinki City Art Museum. *Ana Mendieta, 1948–1985.* Helsinki: Helsinki City Art
Museum, 1996.

Henry Street Settlement. *Exchanges* 1. New York: Henry Street Settlement, Louis Abrons Arts for Living Center, 1979.

———. *Window to the South: Works by Fourteen Contemporary Artists from Latin America.* New York: Henry Street Settlement/Solidaridad Humana, 1979.

Hess, Elizabeth. "The Guggenheim Reborn: Downtown." *Village Voice,* 7 July 1992, p. 87.

Jacob, Mary Jane. In *Ana Mendieta: The "Silueta" Series, 1973–1980.* New York: Galerie Lelong, 1991.

Junod, Henri. *The Life of a South African Tribe.* 1912. New Hyde Park, N.Y.: University Books, 1962.

Kaplan, Caren. "Deterritorializations: The Rewriting of Home and Exile in Western Feminist Discourse." *Cultural Critique* 6 (Spring 1987): 187–98.

Katz, Robert. *Naked by the Window: The Fatal Marriage of Carl Andre and Ana Mendieta.* New York: Atlantic Monthly Press, 1990.

Knafo, Danielle. "In Her Own Image: Self-Representation in the Art of Frida Kahlo and Ana Mendieta." *Art Criticism* 11, no. 2 (Spring 1996): 1–19.

Kristeva, Julia. *Strangers to Ourselves.* Translated by Leon S. Roudiez. New York: Columbia University Press, 1991.

Kwon, Miwon. "Bloody Valentines: Afterimages by Ana Mendieta." In *Inside the Visible: An Elliptical Traverse of 20th Century Art in, of, and from the Feminine,* ed. M. Catherine de Zegher. Cambridge, Mass.: MIT Press, 1996.

Lauter, Estella. *Women as Mythmakers: Poetry and Visual Art by Twentieth Century Women.* Bloomington: Indiana University Press, 1984.

Leiss, William. *The Domination of Nature.* New York: George Braziller, 1972.

Lévy-Bruhl, Lucien. *The Primitive Mentality.* Translated by Lilian A. Clare. New York: Macmillan, 1923.

Lindsay, Arturo, ed. *Santería Aesthetics in Contemporary Latin American Art.* Washington, D.C.: Smithsonian Institution Press, 1996.

Lippard, Lucy R. *From the Center: Feminist Essays on Women's Art.* New York: E. P. Dutton, 1974.

———. "The Pains and Pleasures of Rebirth: Women's Body Art." *Art in America,* May–June 1976, pp. 73–81.

———. "Transformation Art." *Ms,* May–June 1976, pp. 73–81.

———. "Art Outdoors, in and out of the Public Domain: A Slide Lecture." *Studio International,* March/April 1977, pp. 83–90.

———. "Quite Contrary: Body, Nature, Ritual in Women's Art." *Chrysalis,* no. 2 (1977): 31–47.

———. *Overlay: Contemporary Art and the Art of Prehistory.* New York: Pantheon, 1983.

———. "Ana Mendieta, 1948–1985." *Art in America,* November 1985, p. 190.

———. "Cultural Exchange: Made in the USA: Art from Cuba." *Art in America,* April 1986, pp. 27–35.

———. *Mixed Blessings: New Art in a Multicultural America.* New York: Pantheon, 1990.

Livingston, Jane, and John Beardsley. "The Poetics and Politics of Hispanic Art: A

New Perspective." In *Exhibiting Cultures: The Poetics and Politics of Museum Display*, ed. Ivan Karp and Steven D. Levine. Washington, D.C.: Smithsonian Institution Press, 1991.

Lubell, Ellen. "Ana Mendieta at Yvonne Seguy." *Art in America*, Summer 1983, pp. 161.

Martí, José. *Martí on the U.S.A.* Translated by Luis A. Baralt. Carbondale: Southern Illinois University Press, 1966.

————. *En Los Estados Unidos*. Madrid: Alianza Editorial, 1968.

Martínez-Alier, Verena. *Marriage, Class and Colour in Nineteenth Century Cuba: A Study of Racial Attitudes and Sexual Values in a Slave Society*. Cambridge: Cambridge University Press, 1974.

Maryland Institute College of Art. *Rejoining the Spiritual: The Land in Contemporary Latin American Art*. Baltimore, 1994.

Masud-Piloto, Félix Roberto. *With Open Arms: Cuban Migration to the United States*. Totowa, N.J.: Rowman & Littlefield, 1988.

Mendieta, Ana. "Self Portraits." Master's thesis, University of Iowa, 1972.

————. "Venus Negra, Based on a Cuban Legend." *Heresies* 4, no. 1 (1981): 22.

Mendieta Costa, Raquel (Kaki). "Silhouette." Translated by David Frye. *Michigan Quarterly Review* 33, no. 3 (Summer 1994): 548–52.

Mendieta Harrington, Raquel. "Ana Mendieta: Self Portrait of a Goddess." *Review: Latin American Literature and Arts* 39 (January–June 1988): 38–39.

Mexican Museum. *Ceremony of Spirit: Nature and Memory in Contemporary Latino Art*. San Francisco, 1993.

Milwaukee Art Museum. *Latin American Women Artists, 1915–1995*. Milwaukee, 1995.

Moore, Carlos. "Congo or Carabali? Race Relations in Socialist Cuba." *Caribbean Review* 15, no. 2 (Spring 1986): 12–15, 43.

Mosquera, Gerardo. "Esculturas Rupestres de Ana Mendieta." *Arieto* 7, no. 28 (1981): 54–56.

————. *Exploraciones en la plastica cubana*. Havana: Editorial Letras Cubanas, 1983.

————. "New Cuban Art: Identity and Popular Culture." *Art Criticism* 6 (1989): 57–65.

Moure, Gloria, ed. *Ana Mendieta*. Barcelona: Fundació Antoni Tàpies; Santiago de Compostela: Centro Galego de Arte Contemporánea, 1996.

Museum of Contemporary Hispanic Art et al. *The Decade Show: Frameworks of Identity in the 1980s*. New York: Museum of Contemporary Hispanic Art/New Museum of Contemporary Art/Studio Museum of Harlem, 1990.

National Public Radio. "Proposed Border Fence Meets with Opposition and Support." *Weekend Edition Saturday*, 5 February 1994.

New Museum of Contemporary Art. *Ana Mendieta: A Retrospective*. New York: New Museum of Contemporary Art, 1987.

Omi, Michael, and Howard Winant. *Racial Formation in the United States from the 1960s to the 1980s*. New York: Routledge & Kegan Paul, 1986.

Orenstein, Gloria Feman. "The Reemergence of the Archetype of the Great Goddess in Art by Contemporary Women." *Heresies* 2, no. 1 (Spring 1978): 74–84. Reprinted in *Feminist Art Criticism: An Anthology,* ed. Arlene Raven, Cassandra Langer, and Joanna Frueh (Ann Arbor, Mich.: UMI Research Press, 1988).

Ortiz, Fernando. *Cuban Counterpoint: Tobacco and Sugar.* Translated by Harriet de Onis. New York: Alfred A. Knopf, 1947.

———. *El engaño de las razas.* Havana: Editorial de Ciencias Sociales, 1975.

Ortner, Sherry. "Is Female to Male as Nature Is to Culture?" *Feminist Studies* 1, no. 2 (1972): 5–31. Reprinted in *Woman, Culture and Society,* ed. Michelle Rosaldo and Louise Lamphere. (Stanford, Calif.: Stanford University Press, 1974).

Osgood, Cornelius. "The Ciboney Culture of Cayo Redondo, Cuba." *Yale University Publications in Anthropology,* nos. 25–26 (1942): 5–71.

Paquette, Robert L. *Sugar Is Made with Blood: The Conspiracy of La Escalera in the Conflict between Empires over Slavery in Cuba.* Middletown, Conn.: Wesleyan University Press, 1988.

Paz, Octavio. *The Labyrinth of Solitude: Life and Thought in Mexico.* Translated by Lysander Kemp. New York: Grove, 1961.

Perrin, Marlene J. "Ana Mendieta Works with Nature to Produce Her Art." *Iowa City Press Citizen,* 2 December 1977, p. 5A.

Phelan, Peggy. *Unmarked: The Politics of Performance.* New York: Routledge, 1993.

Poggi, Christine. "The New Spiritualism." *Women Artists News,* Summer 1980, p. 6.

Rasmussen, Waldo, ed. *Latin American Artists of the Twentieth Century.* New York: Museum of Modern Art, 1993.

Retamar, Roberto Fernández. *Caliban and Other Essays.* Translated by Edward Baker. Minneapolis: University of Minnesota Press, 1989.

Rich, Adrienne. "Compulsory Heterosexuality and Lesbian Existence." *Signs* 5, no. 4 (Summer 1980): 631–60.

Rich, B. Ruby. "The Screaming Silence." *Village Voice,* 16–23 September 1986, pp. 23–24.

Rosaldo, Michelle. "The Use and Abuse of Anthropology: Reflections on Feminism and Cross-Cultural Understanding." *Signs* 5, no. 3 (Spring 1980): 389–417.

Roth, Moira, ed. *The Amazing Decade: Women and Performance Art in America, 1970–1980.* Los Angeles: Astro Artz, 1983.

Said, Edward. "The Mind of Winter: Reflections on Exile." *Harper's,* September 1984, pp. 49–55.

Sayre, Henry. *The Object of Performance: The American Avant-Garde since 1970.* Chicago: University of Chicago Press, 1989.

Schjeldahl, Peter. "The Guggenheim Reborn: Uptown." *Village Voice,* 7 July 1992, p. 86.

Schneider, Rebecca. *The Explicit Body in Performance.* London: Routledge, 1997.

Schor, Mira. *Wet: On Painting, Feminism, and Art Culture.* Durham, N.C.: Duke University Press, 1997.

Schor, Naomi, and Elizabeth Weed, eds. *The Essential Difference*. Bloomington: Indiana University Press, 1994.

Shepherd, Paul. *Man in the Landscape: A Historic View of the Aesthetics of Nature*. College Station: Texas A&M University Press, 1991.

Sjöö, Monica, and Barbara Mor. *The Great Cosmic Mother: Rediscovering the Religion of the Earth*. San Francisco: Harper & Row, 1987.

Sonfist, Alan, ed. *Art in the Land: A Critical Anthology of Environmental Art*. New York: E. P. Dutton, 1983.

Spelman, Elizabeth. *Inessential Woman: Problems of Exclusion in Feminist Thought*. Boston: Beacon, 1988.

Spero, Nancy. "Tracing Ana Mendieta." *Artforum*, April 1992, pp. 75–77.

Spivak, Gayatri Chakravorty. *The Post-Colonial Critic: Interviews, Strategies, Dialogues*. New York: Routledge, 1990.

State University of New York. *Made in the U.S.A.: Art from Cuba*. Old Westbury, N.Y., 1986.

Steward, Julian H., ed. *Handbook of South American Indians*. Vol. 4, no. 143. Washington, D.C.: Smithsonian Institution Bureau of American Ethnology, 1948.

Stone, Merlin. *When God Was a Woman*. New York: Dial, 1976.

Stoops, Susan L., ed. *More than Minimal: Feminism and Abstraction in the '70s*. Waltham, Mass.: Rose Art Museum, Brandeis University, 1996.

Storr, Robert. *Devil on the Stairs: Looking Back on the Eighties*. Philadelphia: Institute of Contemporary Art, University of Pennsylvania, 1991.

Suchlicki, Jaime. *Cuba from Columbus to Castro*. 3d rev. ed. New York: Brassey's, 1990.

Todorov, Tzvetan. *The Conquest of America: The Question of the Other*. Translated by Richard Howard. New York: Harper & Row, 1984.

Trinh T. Minh-ha. *Woman Native Other*. Bloomington: Indiana University Press, 1989.

Tully, Judd. "In Homage to Ana Mendieta." *New Art Examiner*, May 1986, pp. 59–60.

Turner, Victor. *From Ritual to Theatre: The Human Seriousness of Play*. New York: PAJ, 1982.

Valle, Adrian del. *Tradiciones y leyendas de Cienfuegos*. Havana: Sociedad Editorial Cuba Contemporánea, 1919.

Van Den Abbeele, Georges. *Travel as Metaphor: From Montaigne to Rousseau*. Minneapolis: University of Minnesota Press, 1992.

Wadler, Joyce. "A Death in Art." *New York Magazine*, 16 December 1985, pp. 38–46.

Wagley, Charles. "On the Concept of Social Race in the Americas." In *Contemporary Cultures and Societies of Latin America*, ed. Dwight B. Heath and Richard N. Adams. New York: Random House, 1965.

Walsh, Bryan O. "Cuban Refugee Children." *Journal of Inter-American Studies and World Affairs* 13, nos. 3–4 (July–October 1971): 378–415.

Wilson, Judith. "Ana Mendieta Plants Her Garden." *Village Voice*, 13–19 August 1980, p. 71.

INDEX

Jane Blocker is assistant professor of Art History in the School
of Art and Design at Georgia State University.

Library of Congress Cataloging-in-Publication Data
Blocker, Jane.
Where is Ana Mendieta? : identity, performativity, and exile /
Jane Blocker.
p.   cm.
Includes bibliographical references and index.
ISBN 0-8223-2304-4 (cloth). — ISBN 0-8223-2324-9 (pbk.)
1. Mendieta, Ana, 1948–1985 —Criticism and interpretation.
2. Performance art—United States.   3. Feminism in art.
I. Mendieta, Ana, 1948–1985.   II. Title.
NX512.M46B63   1999
709'.2 — dc21   98-30341   CIP